T0369580

Private International Law

Private International Law

A Case Study

V.C. GOVINDARAJ

OXFORD
UNIVERSITY PRESS

OXFORD
UNIVERSITY PRESS

Oxford University Press is a department of the University of Oxford.
It furthers the University's objective of excellence in research, scholarship,
and education by publishing worldwide. Oxford is a registered trademark of
Oxford University Press in the UK and in certain other countries.

Published in India by
Oxford University Press
2/11 Ground Floor, Ansari Road, Daryaganj, New Delhi 110 002, India

ISBN-13: 978-0-19-948928-2
ISBN-10: 0-19-948928-9

Typeset in Trump Mediaeval LT Std 9.5/13.7
by Tranistics Data Technologies, Kolkata 700 091
Printed in India by Rakmo Press, New Delhi 110 020

I hereby dedicate this, my case study on private international law, to the legal community who shall ever be instrumental in upholding the rule of law and the rights and interests of people.

CONTENTS

PREFACE

In 2011, the author had published a textbook on Conflict of Laws (also known as Private International Law), titled *The Conflict of Laws in India: Inter-Territorial and Inter-Personal Conflict*, with Oxford University Press. It was followed by a concise rendering of the same, designed for use by students of law as well as scholars and practitioners of law. Having witnessed the impressive circulation of the above two texts, the author feels encouraged to bring out a case-book that will be particularly helpful for senior practitioners of law and judges of High Courts and the Supreme Court. The author, at the same time, feels constrained to admit whether his wish or expectations may come true with this, the third of his contribution that highlights the basics of the science of Conflict of Laws.

Judges of the superior courts in India lean heavily on English case-law and on the views of renowned English jurists, like Professors A.V. Dicey and G.C. Cheshire, in deciding cases on Conflict of Laws. The time has come to evolve our own system of Conflict of Laws as did the American Courts and American jurists in the course of the last two hundred years. In fact, the United States of America outclassed the United Kingdom in coming forward with three re-statements in the course of the twentieth century, each one of them separated by thirty years.

Recently there was a get-together in the Indian Law Institute, New Delhi, to have a discussion on the need for restating the Indian Conflict of Laws. I may, with due apologies, suggest that we may have to learn to state the law before we cherish the desire to go for a re-statement of the Indian Conflict of Laws. Under the circumstances, the author felt the need to bring out a case-book on Indian Conflict of Laws that may, hopefully, lead to the cherished desire to evolve and then go for a restatement of our own system of Conflict of Laws.

The author, in this work, has dealt with cases that call for comment in the three main areas of the subject, namely, the law of obligations, the law of persons, and the law of property, besides cases that call for comment in respect of foreign judgments and foreign arbitral awards, as also the laws relating to procedure.

The author acknowledges with gratitude the good wishes and encouragement that he got in abundance from friends and well-wishers. The author owes a deep debt of gratitude to his friend Mr Amresh Chadha who, despite his other commitments, social and official, found time to type out this work on the computer.

11 June 2018   V.C. GOVINDARAJ

TABLE OF CASES

BRIEF OUTLINE FOR
THE CASE STUDY

———

Conflict of Laws or Private International Law, as it is also
known, is a tough branch of jurisprudence. Transactions
across frontiers in the globalized village we live in are
so frequent and so numerous that courts of law, and, in
particular, the higher judiciary, namely the Supreme Court
and the High Courts, are called upon to resolve them in
order to render justice to the parties before them.

In the absence of legislations, not to talk of codification
of Conflict of Laws, courts of law are obligated to resolve
them. In that sense, this branch of law is virtually
judge-made. Unlike other countries, where conflicts are
inter-territorial, in the Indian sub-continent conflicts
are also inter-personal in that our various religious
communities have their own systems of law to regulate
their relationships. To usher in a uniform civil code in

accordance with Article 44 of the Directive Principles of State Policy of Chapter 4 of the Constitution of India is therefore a far cry.

Unlike other advanced countries like the United states and the United Kingdom, we suffer from a dearth of legal writings in Conflict of Laws that cast a burden on the judges of the Superior Courts to fall back upon their own notions of conflict resolution. This often results in bizarre ratio that they employ based, predominantly, on English case law.

We are hopeful that this casebook will be of immense help to the higher judiciary in India in resolving disputes, whether inter-territorial or inter-personal. It may also render help to the legal community in guiding the judiciary to resolve disputes on Conflict of Laws.

Part I

DOMICILE AND RESIDENCE

———

The concept of domicile in Conflict of Laws is, to say the least, most nebulous and intriguing. It is left to the courts to elicit the domicile of a person by probing into his/her life as to where the concerned wanted to set up a home. Apparently, the concept of domicile looks simple. It only calls for the determination the *factum* of residence coupled with *animus* or the intension of the concerned that constitutes domicile, *animo et facto* as it is called. But, in reality, it is not as simple as it appears to be. There are English cases, like *Winans v. A.G., 1904, AC 287,* and *Ramsey v. Liverpool Royal Infirmary, 1930, SC (HL) 8,* where residence for life failed to confer a domicile on the concerned. There are, at the same time, cases where a fleeting residence bestowed on the concerned domicile. As irony would have it, we have cases like the English case, *in re* O' Keefe, where the court imposed upon a lady a domicile in a country where she never resided, based upon her father's domicile which, ironically enough, was imposed upon her by the court as her domicile of origin. The reviewer chose in this Case Study to deal with select leading Indian cases to highlight the concept of domicile.

We have, in this part, a case-law to establish that the Union of India is uni-domiciliary and not multi-domiciliary, even though legislatures of States constituting the Union of India are accorded legislative competence to enact laws in the State List and Concurrent List of the Seventh Schedule of the Constitution of India.

Central Bank of India, Petitioner v. Ram Narain, Respondent, AIR 1955, 36; 1955 SCR (1) 697

This case is a classic example to elucidate what the concept of domicile means from a legal standpoint. Lord Cranworth in his judgment in the case *Whicker v. Hume (1858), 7 H.L.C. 124, 160*, uttered the following words in a light vein to elucidate the concept of domicile. It runs thus:

By domicile we mean home, the permanent home, and if you do not understand your permanent home I'm afraid that no illustrations drawn from foreign writers will help you to it.

Five years later, that is, in the year 1863, His Lordship in the case *Moorhouse v. Lord (1863), 10 H.L.C. 272, 285–6* attempted a legal definition of the concept of domicile as set out below:

The present intention of making a place a person's permanent home can exist only where he has no other idea than to continue there, without looking forward to any other event, certain or uncertain, which might induce him to change his residence. If he has in his contemplation some event upon the happening of which his residence will cease, it is not correct to call this even a present intention of making it a permanent home. It is rather a present intention of making it a temporary home, though for a period indefinite and contingent.

Seventy-three years before Lord Cranworth attempted a legal definition of domicile in the case *Moorhouse v. Lord, 1863, 10 HLC 272*, as set out above, Lord Thurlow raised a query in the case *Bruce v. Bruce (1790), 2 Bos. and Pul 229*, simplistic though it may seem to be, which runs thus: 'A British man settles as a merchant abroad; he enjoys the privileges of the place; he may mean to return when he has made his fortune; but if he dies in the interval will it be maintained that he had his domicile at home'.

However, Lord Cranworth's definition of the concept of domicile seems to be vindicated in the light of two leading decisions of the House of Lords, namely, *Winans v. A.G (1904) A.C. 287* and *Ramsay v. Liverpool Royal Infirmary (1939) A.C. 588*.

With this prefatory note, based on the English Conflict of Laws, a fruitful attempt can be made to review the decision in the leading Indian case on domicile, namely, *Central Bank of India v. Ram Narain*.

The facts of the case, briefly stated, are as follows:

The respondent Ram Narain was doing business at Mailsi in the district of Multan, his ancestral home, which, after the partition of British India in August 1947 as Dominion of India and Dominion of Pakistan became part of Pakistan. He was carrying on business at Mailsi under the name and style Ram Narain Joginder Nath; the firm had a cash credit arrangement with the Mailsi branch of the Central Bank of India to the tune of three lakhs on

23 December 1946 shortly before the partition of British India. The amount due to the Ram Narain was to the tune of Rs 1,40,000, exclusive of interest, while the value of the goods pledged under the cash credit agreement was approximately in the sum of Rs 1,90,000. The account was secured against stocks of 801 cotton bales which were to remain in possession of the borrowers as trustees on behalf of the bank. In the wake of disturbances that occurred during the partition of British India, the godown keeper at Mailse had to flee from there in September 1947 and the cashier, who was left in charge also had to leave that place in October 1947, that resulted in the bales of cotton pledged to their own fate. It was alleged that when the agent of the bank, Mr D.P. Patel, visited the godown at Mailsi, he found that the stocks of 801 cotton bales pledged by Ram Narain Joginder Nath under the cash credit arrangement with the bank had disappeared. On inquiry he learnt that 801 bales of cotton pledged by Messrs. Ram Narain Joginder Nath against the cash credit agreement had been stolen by Ram Narain and booked by him to Karachi on 9 November 1947, and passed on to one Durgadas D. Punjabi for a sum of Rs 1,98,702-12-9. The bank's attempt to recover the money due to it from Ram Narain proved infructuous. It, then, sought the permission of the East Punjab Government for sanction to prosecute Ram Narain under Section 188 of the Criminal Procedure Code for the offence committed by him in Pakistan in November 1947, when he was there in respect of the 801 bales of cotton. The East of Punjab Government, by its order dated the 23 February 1950, accorded sanction to prosecute Ram Narain under Sections 380 and 454 of the Indian Penal Code. Ram Narain, at that time, was residing at Hodel in the district of Gurgaon and was carrying on business under the name and style of Ram Narain Bhola Nath, Hodel. The bank

filed a complaint against Ram Narain in pursuance of the sanction on 18 April 1950, under Sections 380 and 454 as also under Section 412 of the Indian Penal Code before the district magistrate of Gurgaon.

Ram Narain countered the criminal prosecution launched against him by raising a preliminary objection, namely, that at the time of the alleged occurrence, he was a national of Pakistan and, as such, the East Punjab Government was not competent to grant the said sanction to prosecute him under Section 188 of the Criminal Procedure Code as read with Section 4 of the Indian Penal Code. The district magistrate, who, understandably, cannot be credited with knowledge of Conflict of Laws, overruled Ram Narain's preliminary objection by holding that he could not be credited with a Pakistan nationality by his merely staying on there from 15 August till 10 November 1947, in view of Ram Narain's intention to revert to Indian nationality, which was further strengthened by his family being sent to India in October 1947, coupled with his winding up of his business and taking up residence at Hodel in the district of Gurgaon, where he set up the business designated Ram Narain Bhola Nath, Hodel. He also averred that he never set foot in Pakistan after his migration to India in November 1947. Further, it was well known that Hindus and Sikhs in those days were not safe in Pakistan and that they were bound to come to India under the unavoidable pressure of circumstances over which they had no control. Thereupon, Ram Narain preferred an appeal to the Additional District Judge at Gurgaon under Sections 435 and 439 of the Criminal Procedure Code for setting aside the said order of the Hon'ble Magistrate and for quashing the charges framed against him. The Hon'ble Additional Judge dismissed the petition and affirmed the decision of the trial magistrate.

Ram Narain then preferred an application in revision to the Punjab High Court at Shimla which allowed the revision petition and quashed the charges, holding thereby that the trial of the respondent Ram Narain by a magistrate in India was without jurisdiction. It was also held by the High Court that until Ram Narain actually left Pakistan and came to India, he could not be credited with any acquisition of 'Indian citizenship' or, as the case may be, of Indian domicile. This despite the fact that he never intended to remain in Pakistan for any length of time in view of the fact that he wound up his business at Mailsi as expeditiously as he could and came to India in November 1947, and settled down in Hodel. Besides, the High Court also held that the East Punjab Government had no power in February 1950 to sanction his prosecution under Section 188 of the Criminal Procedure Code for acts committed by him in Pakistan in November 1947. Besides, the High Court repelled the further contention of the appellant that the possession or retention by Ram Narain at Hodel, Gurgaon, of the sale proceeds of the stolen cotton would virtually constitute stolen property. Leave to appeal to the Supreme Court was granted by the Punjab High Court under Article 134 (1) (C) of the Constitution of India. The one and only legal issue that called for determination by the Supreme Court in this appeal is, whether on a true construction of Section 188 of the Criminal Procedure as read with Section 4 of the Indian Penal Code, the East Punjab Government had the power to grant sanction to prosecute Ram Narain for the offence of stealing 801 bales of cotton pledged by Messrs. Ram Narain Joginder Nath against the cash credit agreement entered between him and the Central Bank of India at Mailsi in the district of Multan.

The Supreme Court, speaking through Mr Justice Mehr Chand Mahajan analysed the factual situation in the case with a view to find out where Ram Narain was domiciled at the time when he committed the offence in November 1947. His contention of dispatching his family to India in October 1947, and he too, leaving Mailsi for good to take up residence at Hodel in the district of Gurgaon in India on the 10 November 1947 would render his acquisition of Indian domicile and Indian citizenship a *fait accompli*, was summarily dismissed as unworthy of consideration. Yet another argument of the Attorney–General on behalf of the appellant bank, namely that Ram Narain could be prosecuted at Gurgaon for the possession or retention by him at Hodel of the sale proceeds of the stolen cotton was rejected by Mr Justice Mehr Chand Mahajan in no uncertain terms as did the Punjab High Court in the revision petition presented before it. The learned judge falls back upon the definition given by Mr Justice Chitty in *Craignish v. Craignish* for the expression 'domcil', which runs thus: 'That place is properly the domicil of a person in which his habitation is fixed without any present intention of removing therefrom'. But he admits, however, that the above definition is not absolute in that the term 'domicil' could only be illustrated, but not defined. He adverts to the well-established proposition that a person may have no home but he cannot be without a domicil, and that the law may attribute to him a domicil in a country where in reality he has not. 'Domicil' is acquired by a person by residing in a country coupled with an intention of making it his permanent home. As the saying goes, acquisition of domicil calls for *animo et facto*. The learned judge ratiocinates that Ram Narain could not be credited with any acquisition of Indian domicile at the time when he committed the offence. Accordingly, for the reasons stated above, he concludes that the decision of the High Court of Punjab that Ram Narain could not be tried in any court in India for the offence committed by him at Mailsi in November 1947, is right and that the Provincial Government had no power whatsoever under Section 188 of the Criminal Procedure Code to accord sanction for his prosecution at Hodel in the district of Gurgaon in India.

In conclusion, the learned judge could be credited with adopting a cogent ratio in his upholding the judgment of the Punjab High Court in dismissing the appeal. However, he could have well avoided any reference to Ram Narain's alleged acquisition of Indian citizenship, in much as the common law countries, to which India belongs, fall back upon *lex domicilii*, and not *lex patriae*, for judging the permanent home of an individual which was in contention.

Sharafat Ali Khan, Petitioner v. State of Uttar Pradesh, Respondent, AIR 1960, Allahabad, 687

This case calls for no more than a passing reference, in that it emphasizes the basic norm that the law imposes on an individual, a domicil in a country which, in reality, he has no domicil in.

The facts, briefly stated, are as follows:

The petitioner, an Indian citizen at birth, went to Pakistan when he was still a minor. His father, a natural guardian, remained in India with his family which speaks for his retention of Indian domicil and citizenship. His father was murdered in India after the petitioner attained majority. It is but natural, therefore, that he was impelled to return to India to take care of his widowed mother and his younger brother and sisters. He was, therefore, compelled to seek and obtain a Pakistani passport and also a visa from the Indian High Commissioner in Pakistan that facilitated his return to India. From a legal standpoint, the petitioner's seeking and obtaining a Pakistani passport after attaining majority would impose upon him a Pakistani nationality with the resulting consequence of his forfeiting his Indian citizenship as per Section 9 (1) of the Indian Citizenship Act.

The High Court of Allahabad ignored the arbitrary rule laid down in clause 8 of Schedule III of the Citizenship Rule, 1956, and held that the petitioner was compelled to embrace Pakistani citizenship under stress for seeking and obtaining a Pakistani passport that led to the termination of his Indian citizenship under the said Section 9 (1) of the Indian Citizenship Act. Therefore, under the circumstance of the case, the mere obtaining of the Pakistani passport by the petitioner should not be construed as any acquisition by him of a Pakistani citizenship. Accordingly, the petitioner's declaration in his application seeking a Pakistani passport that he was a Pakistani citizen could at best be nothing more than an admission which was capable of being explained away (see Cri. Rev. No. 631 of 1959, D-7-3-1960 (All), Foll).

The following observation of Mister Justice W. Broom, J. that led to the decision stated above calls for reproduction. It runs thus:

In the circumstances, to suggest to the petitioner that he has the alternative remedy of making an application to the Central Government would be no more reasonable than to tell him that he has the alternative remedy of committing suicide. I am satisfied therefore that there is no other equally efficacious and convenient remedy available to the petitioner and conclude that there is no bar to the issue of a writ in his favour.

The petitioner's application was, accordingly, allowed with costs. A writ of mandamus was issued directing the opposite parties to forbear from enforcing the orders requiring the petitioner to leave the territory of India.

The State, Appellant v. Naryandas Mangilal Dayame, Respondent, AIR 1958, Bombay 68

This Full Bench decision of the Bombay High Court, one of the earliest of its kind, examines the question whether the Union of India is uni-domiciliary or multi-domiciliary. This question arises because the Union of India consists of States which are invested with competence to enact laws in the State List and in the Concurrent List of the Seventh Schedule of the Constitution of India. All the same, if there is a conflict between a Union law and a State law, the Union law prevails (see Article 254, Part XI of the Constitution). The facts of the case, briefly stated, are as follows:

The respondent, the accused in this case, was married in Bombay in 1948. On 16 May 1955, he entered into a second marriage with yet another lady at Bikaner. Prior to the passing of the Hindu Marriage Act, 1955, the Hindu law permitted polygamy. The Province of Bombay enacted the Bombay Prevention of Hindu Bigamous Marriage Act, Act 25 of 1946, forbidding polygamy and making it an offence. On 5 July his first wife lodged a complaint against her husband with the First Class Judicial Magistrate at Sholapur. The learned magistrate acquitted the accused on the ground that the prosecution that was launched after Act 25 of 1946 was repealed by the Central Act 25 of 1955 which came into force on 18 May 1955. The State of Bombay preferred an appeal against the acquittal order of the learned magistrate. As the Division Bench of the Bombay High Court had doubts about the reliability of its earlier decision in the case *Radhabai Mohandas v. Bombay State, AIR 1955, Bombay 439*, in respect of the Bombay Act and its applicability to marriages contracted outside the State of Bombay, the question was referred to a Full Bench.

The High Court of Bombay, speaking through Mr Justice Chagla, the Chief Justice of the Bombay High Court, dismissed the appeal preferred by the State, thereby upholding the order of acquittal of the accused by the learned magistrate, Sholapur, though not for the reasons stated by him.

The issue before the Court was whether the Bombay Legislature had the competence under the Constitution of India to enact the Bombay Act 25 of 1946, giving it extra-territorial operation. As stated earlier, the respondent was prosecuted under the Act for his committing the offence of bigamy by his entering into a second marriage at Bikaner. The learned magistrate acquitted the accused on the ground, as stated earlier, that the prosecution was launched after the Bombay Act 25 of 1946 was repealed by the Union Parliament by the passing of the Central Act 25 of 1955 which came into force on 18 May 1955. Obviously, the learned magistrate could not be credited with knowledge of Conflict of Laws for him to base his acquittal order on the ground that India is uni-domiciliary and, as such, the Bombay Legislative lacked legislative competence to enact the said Act giving it extra-territorial operation.

Mister Justice Chagla, after having defined the concept of 'domicil' for the acquisition of which it requires residence by the concerned in the country, coupled with his intention to make his residence permanent, that is, *animo et facto* as the saying goes in Latin. The learned judge recalls Halsbury's version of domicil which runs thus: 'A person's domicile is that country in which he either has or is deemed by laws to have his permanent home' (Vol. 6, page 198, Art. 242).

Halsbury, in the same paragraph, elaborates the definition of domicile as, 'All those persons who have, or whom the law deems to have, their permanent home within the territorial limits of a single system of law are domiciled in the country over which the system extends; and they are domiciled in the whole of that country, although their home may be fixed at a particular spot within it'.

On the strength of the above definition of Halsbury, Mr Justice Chagla ratiocinates thus:

Now, in our opinion, it is a total misapprehension of the position in law in our country to talk of a person being domiciled in a Province or in a State. A person can only be domiciled in India as a whole. That is the only country that can be considered in the context of the expression 'domicile' and the only system of law by which a person is governed in India is the system of law which prevails in the whole country and not any system of law which prevails in any Province or State.... Therefore, in India we have one citizenship, the citizenship of India. We have one domicile— the domicile in India and we have one legal system—the system that prevails in the whole country. The most that we can say about a person in a State is that he is permanently resident in a particular State. But, as Halsbury points out, to which we have made reference, the mere fact that a man's home may be fixed at a particular spot within the country does not make him domiciled in the whole country, and therefore, whether a man permanently resides in Bombay or Madras or Bengal or anywhere does not make him domiciled in Bombay, Madras or Bengal but makes him domiciled in India; Bombay, Madras and Bengal being particular spots in India as a country.

Accordingly, Mr Justice Chagla points out how the misconception of provincial or state domicile had arisen in our legal system and the need to rid the Indian Conflict of Laws from such misconception. He reasons out as set out below:

Any law passed by a State Legislature can be applied to any person within the State, and therefore the expression 'domicile' has no relevance whatever in construing the competency of the State Legislature. If the State Legislature is legislating on a topic within its competence, that law can be made applicable to anyone in the State of Bombay whether he is a resident or not or even if he is a foreigner passing through the State of Bombay. Therefore, it is fallacious to suggest that the doctrine of domicile is introduced in our law by reason of the fact that the State or Provincial Legislature has been given the power to legislate with regard to certain subject-matters within the territorial ambit. It, therefore, seems to us that the expression 'domicile' used in any State or Provincial law is a misnomer and it does not carry with the implications which that expression has when used in the context of International Law.

The controversy whether India is uni-domiciliary or multi-domiciliary, which was set at naught in the case, *the State v. Narayandas Mangilal Dayame, 1958, Bombay 68 (V 45)*, arose for consideration in an earlier case, *Kamlabai v. Devram Sona Bodgujar, AIR 1955, Bombay 300*. This was a case where the respondent Devram, a habitual resident of Madhya Pradesh, married the appellant Kamlabai, a resident of Amalner in the State of Bombay, in Madhya Pradesh in the year 1945 which proved to be a failure even from the start. The respondent, therefore, was constrained to take another wife in 1952. The appellant filed a plaint before the district judge at Dhulia, pleading that the second marriage by her husband was in contravention of the Bombay Hindu Divorce Act (22 of 1947) and, accordingly, sought leave to sue her husband under Section 5 (3) of the Bombay Act for divorce and alimony. But it was refused by the District Judge. On her appeal to the High Court of Bombay, the Court, speaking through Mr Justice Gajendragadkar, dismissed the appeal on the ground that the Bombay Act could not have extra-territorial operation. The learned judge ratiocinates thus:

[I]t cannot be disputed that on marriage the wife takes the domicile of the husband and it is common ground that the husband has always been a resident of Madhya Pradesh and not of the State of Bombay. Therefore, it seems to me that the learned District Judge was right in holding that the marriage between the plaintiff and the defendant could not claim the protection of the Bombay Hindu Divorce Act, 1947.

The reviewer is constrained to reiterate that India is uni-domiciliary and not multi-domiciliary even though the legislatures of States constituting the Union of India are accorded legislative competence to enact laws in the State List and the Concurrent List of the Seventh Schedule of the Constitution of India.

In yet another case, namely, *Parwathawwa v. Channawwa, AIR 1966, Mysore 100*, it was a dispute of succession to the property of one Siddhalingiah, who, before the coming into force of the Constitution of India, 1950, married Channawwa, a permanent resident of Bombay. Siddhalingiah himself being domiciled in the erstwhile independent State of Hyderabad. Siddhalingiah was already married before entering into marriage with Channawwa. In the succession dispute the validity of the second marriage of Channawwa was raised in that the said marriage was in contravention of the Bombay Prevention of Hindu Bigamous Marriage Act. As one would expect, the Mysore High Court ought to have dismissed the contention on the ground that the said Act of Bombay could not be credited with extra-territorial operation. Strange as it may seem, the Mysore High Court, speaking through Mr Justice Somnath Iyer, talks of the determination of the validity or otherwise of the marriage based on the intended matrimonial home theory, as opposed to the dual domicile doctrine. This clearly shows that the learned judge was oblivious to the legal norm that India is uni-domiciliary and not multi-domiciliary.

Part II

THE LAW OF OBLIGATIONS

Foreign Contracts and Foreign Torts

———

Professor A.V. Dicey, England, and Professor Joseph Beale, United States of America, have both adopted the jurisdiction selection rule to govern the Law of Obligations, whether it be a foreign contract or a foreign tort. In respect of a foreign contract, the governing law is the law of the place where the contract is entered into or, as the case may be, where its performance is due. Similarly, the law to govern a foreign tort is the law of the place where the tort is committed. This simplistic approach of Dicey and Beale does not reflect their judicial determination by courts of law. Appropriately, therefore, Professor J.H.C. Morris adopted the proper law doctrine to govern cases relating to foreign contracts or foreign torts with a view to achieve results which, in his own words, are 'commercially convenient and sound for the determination of the law to govern a foreign contract, or, as the case may be, 'socially convenient and sound' to govern a foreign tort'.

This approach of Professor J.H.C. Morris finds its reflection in the cases that the reviewer has taken up as illustrative in the case study.

The Law of Obligations—Foreign Contracts

The Delhi Cloth and General Mills Co. Ltd. v. Harnam Singh and Other Respondents, AIR 1955, SC 590

This is a classic decision in the law relating to foreign contracts, based on the 'proper law' doctrine of Professor J.H.C. Morris, for resolution of disputes relating the law of obligations, consisting of contracts and torts, with a view to achieving results which, according to Morris, are 'commercially convenient and sound' in respect of contracts and 'socially convenient and sound' in respect of torts.

The facts of the case, briefly stated, are as follows:

During the Second World War cloth was being rationed by the government through government nominees and other authorized persons at Lyallpur, then a part of the Punjab in the undivided India. Harnam Singh and others, the plaintiffs-respondents, had entered into a contract with the defendant company, the Delhi Cloth and General Mills Ltd. at its branch at Lyallpur and supplied cloth from time to time, in conformity with the government quota, through its branch manager at Lyallpur.

Their dealings lasted some four or five years prior to 1947. The plaintiff's company left a security deposit of Rs 1,000 with the defendant's manager at Lyallpur, besides depositing further sums of money from time to time as and when required. After the partition of India, two independent states emerged, namely, India and Pakistan. The plaintiffs, thereupon, fled from Lyallpur and became evacuees in Delhi. The Government of Pakistan then issued an ordinance vesting the assets and money at the disposal of the plaintiffs' company at Lyallpur, including the security deposit, in the custodian of evacuee property in Pakistan. Thereupon, the deputy custodian of evacuee property demanded payment of moneys from the defendant that he owed to plaintiffs. After some correspondence and demur, the payment was made as required. The defendant pleaded this as a defence to the action.

While allowing the appeal filed by the defendant company, the Delhi Cloth and General Mills Ltd., the Supreme Court, speaking through Mr Justice Vivian Bose, held as follows:

(1) Lyallpur was the place of primary obligation, because under the contract the balance remaining at its termination was to be paid there and not elsewhere; accordingly, the demand for payment made at Delhi before a demand and refusal at Lyallpur was ineffective.

(2) The elements that constituted the contract, giving rise to a legal obligation to pay, were so densely grouped at Lyallpur that it (namely Lyallpur) became the natural seat of the contract with which the densely grouped elements had the closest and the most real connection. Accordingly, the proper law of the contract was the law of Lyallpur.

(3) As per the English Conflict of Laws, too, the *situs* of the debt would be Lyallpur and not Delhi by any stretch of imagination.

(4) Whether it be English or Indian Conflict of Laws, the law of Lyallpur called for application, and that what it

would be at the time of performance with changes, if any, in it. The law of Lyallpur as the proper law of the contract, intended by the parties to govern the contract, was to be administered 'as a living and changing body of law'.

(5) A debt being a chose in action is 'property' within the meaning of the Pakistan Ordinance.

(6) Consequently, the money was rightly paid to the Deputy Custodian of Pakistan which operated as a good discharge and thereby exonerated the defendant from further liability.

But quære, whether different conditions would not arise in a case where no payment was made and the defendant had no garnishable assets in Pakistan out of which the West Punjab government could realize the debt form out of thc defendant's property there.

(7) In conclusion, the learned Mr Justice Vivian Bose holds the view that the provisions of the Pakistan Ordinance relevant to the case are not opposed to the public policy of India and so could be relied on as defence to an action of this nature.

For the reasons set out above, the appeal was allowed.

COMMENTS

The reviewer appreciates the reliance placed by Mr Justice Vivian Bose on two Houses of Lords cases, namely, *Mount Albert Borough Council v. Australasian Temperance and General Mutual Life Assurance Society Ltd. (1938) AC 204A* and *Bonython v. Commonwealth of Australia (1951) AC 201*, for defining the proper law of a contract. According to Lord Wright in the Mount Albert case, the proper law of a contract is 'that law which the English or other court is to apply in determining the obligation under the contract' thus drawing a distinction between obligation and performance. Lord Symonds in the Bonython case defined the proper law as 'the system of law by reference to which the contract was made or that with which the transaction has its closest and most real connection'.[1]

The learned judge makes an observation set out below which is puzzling, to say the least. It runs thus:

We now have to determine the legal liabilities which arise out of these facts. This raises complex questions of Private International Law, and two distinct lines of thought emerge. One is that applied by the English Courts, namely, the *lex situs*; the other is the one favoured by Cheshire in his book on Private International Law, namely, the 'proper law of the contact'.[2]

With due respect to the learned judge, there is no complexity whatsoever in English Conflict of Laws in determining the legal liabilities that a transaction gives rise to.

It may be pointed out, however, that the English Conflict of Laws employs two phrases, namely 'chose in action' and 'chose in possession' which are peculiar to the English system. Chose in action means 'a personal right not reduced into possession, but recoverable by a suit at law....' A right to receive or recover a debt, demand, or damages on a cause of action *ex contractu* or *for a tort*, or omission of a duty (assignable rights of action *ex contractu*, and perhaps *ex delicto*. 'Chose in possession' means a personal thing of which one has possession as distinguished from a thing in action (see Black's Law Dictionary, Revised Fourth Edition, 1968, p. 305).

[1] See V.C. Govindaraj, *The Conflict of Laws in India: Inter-Territorial and Inter-Personal Conflict*, 2011 (New Delhi: Oxford University Press).

[2] See p. 10 of the judgment.

Debt, no doubt, has a *situs*, and the law to govern a debt is the law that governs the contract or the transaction that gave rise to the debt. It is a chose in action and not a chose in possession. As set out earlier, a chose in action may mean a personal right not reduced into possession but recoverable by a suit at law, or may be a debt, demand, or damages on a cause of action *ex contractu* (that is, from or out of a contract). A chose in possession, on the other hand, is a thing in possession of someone, in contradistinction to a thing in action, and as such governed by his *lex domicilii*.

The Supreme Court of India in this case, speaking through Mr Justice Vivian Bose, impliedly considers debt as property, though conceding at the same time that debt is chose in action that inevitably led him to apply the so-called English rule *lex situs* as the governing law which obviously is a misnomer. *Lex situs* is, in fact, applied only to regulate immovable property wherever the parties concerned may have their residence or domicile. The law of the country where the immovable is situated is the law that governs the case whatever may be the intention of the parties, express or implied.

Yet, again, the learned judge attributes the 'proper law of the contract' doctrine to G.C. Cheshire, quoting his fourth edition of the year 1952. The originator of the proper law of the contract doctrine is not Professor Cheshire but Professor J.H.C. Morris. The latter propounded the proper law doctrine when he was a visiting professor at Harvard University Law School. This he did by combining the 'rule selection' rule of Professor Cavers and the issue based approach of Professor Cook for resolving conflicts into a philosophic doctrine of 'proper law' which, in fact, is a generic concept, if I may say so, for resolving disputes in respect of Law of Obligations with a view to achieve results which are 'commercially convenient and sound' in respect of contracts and 'socially convenient and sound' in respect of torts. In fact, courts in England have unreservedly embraced the proper law doctrine of Morris as exemplified in a catena of cases in respect of foreign contracts, the classic instance being the decision of the Houses of Lords in the case of *International Trustee for the Protection of Bond Holders v. R (1936), 52 T.L.R. 82 (1936) 3 ALL. E.R.407.*[3]

A passing reference to the decision of the *Calcutta High Court in Rabindra N. Maitra v. Life Insurance Corporation of India, AIR 1964 Calcutta 141* is called for here. That was a case where the issue that called for determination was the validity of an assignment of an insurance policy, a chose in action, from a father to his son, both residing at Calcutta at the time of assignment, notice of it having been promptly communicated to the Life Insurance Corporation of India, the debtor, with its head office at Bombay and registered with it as required under the Indian Law. However, certain elements relating to the assignment called for consideration of the law of Pakistan. They are as follows:

The father, the assignor, happened to be a permanent resident of Rajshahi which, after the partition of India, became part of Pakistan. The insurance premia ware paid by the assignor in Indian rupees at Rajshahi. The register relating to the insurance policy was kept at Dhaka which was also a part of Pakistan and later became the capital of Bangladesh wherefrom servicing for the insurance policy was provided. The High Court of Calcutta held that the proper law to govern the contract of assignment of the insurance policy was Bombay, that is, the Indian law,

---

[3] See Gonvidaraj, *The Conflict of Laws in India*, p. 55.

where the Head office of the Life Insurance Corporation was located.

Law of Obligation: Foreign Torts

Kotah Transport Limited, Kotah v. Jhalawar Transport Service Limited, AIR 1960 Rajasthan 224: (1960) ILR 10 Raj 705

Three appeals were filed before the High Court of Rajasthan as against the judgments and decrees of the District Court, two from Kotah and one from Jhalawar, in suits filed by passengers or their relatives for deaths and injuries suffered by them due to the collision of the two transport buses, seeking recovery of damages from the defendant, the Kotah Transport Ltd., the appellants in all these three appeals. All three appeals were dismissed by the High Court of Rajasthan, as the High Court found that the award of damages to the victims of the collision by the two District Courts of Kotah and one Civil Court at Jhalawar were well founded, in that the fault was squarely upon the driver of the Kotah transport bus whose rash and negligent driving caused the collision. Both Kotah and Jhalawar were independent States at the time of the collision. The counsel for the appellant, namely, the Kotah Transport Limited contended, based on the so-called double actionability doctrine presumed to have been laid down by Willis, J. in the case *Phillips v. Eyre, (1870) 6 LRQB1*, namely, that in respect of a suit for a tort, committed abroad, two conditions must be satisfied: that it shall be actionable as tort under *lex fori* and that it shall also be actionable as per the *lex loci delicti commissi*. He relied upon Rule 180 of Dicey's Conflict of Laws which runs thus: 'Whether an act done in a foreign country is or is not a tort (i.e. a wrong for which action can be brought in England) depends upon the combined effect of the law of the country where the act is done *(lex loci deliciti commissi)* and of the law of England *(lex fori)'*.

Rule 181 of Dicey further clarifies and provides as follows:

An act done in a foreign country is a tort and actionable as such in England, only if it is both (1) actionable as a tort, according to English law, or, in other words, is an act which, if done in England, would be a tort; and (2) not justifiable, according to the law of the foreign country where it was done.

The full Bench of the Rajasthan High Court, while dismissing the appeal filed by the Kotah Transport Limited, observed as follows:

We have no doubt as to the correctness of the principles embodied in the above rules, and it is manifest that clauses (2) of the rule will govern this case. Here there is nothing to show that the laws of Jhalawar justified such an act. That it was a wrongful act is undoubted, and it could not be justified by any such law. Therefore, it is obvious that the *lex loci delicti commissi* has been established and nothing has been shown to the contrary. The plaintiff would, therefore, be entitled to recover damages. For the above reasons we do not find it possible to entertain the contention of the learned counsel in spite of all his strenuous endeavour to persuade us to do so; that there was no cause of action in favour of the plantiffs, and that the planiffs suit should be thrown out on that account (para 31 of the judgment).

COMMENT

Comment is surely superfluous! One wonders how faithfully the Rajasthan High Court clung to the interpretation and application of the twin criteria laid down by the great judge Willis, J. in the case *Phillips v. Eyre* in the year 1869, namely, the so-called double actionability doctrine, which for nearly 100 years suffered a distortion at the hands of the English courts. What exactly Willis, J. meant by the twin criteria laid down by him in a suit on a foreign tort is that it shall be actionable under the *lex fori*, meaning thereby that the court before which the action for a tort, committed elsewhere, is brought should have jurisdictional competence to entertain the case as per *lex fori*. The said norm is meant to deter forum shopping and adventitiousness. The second criterion is that it shall be actionable in tort as per *lex loci delicti commissi* (that is, the law of the country where the tort is committed).

The classic example of the distortion of the twin criteria laid down by Willis, J. in *Phillips v. Eyre* is the decision of the Queen Bench Division in *Machado v. Fontes (1897) 2 QB231*. That was a case brought before an English court for a libel published by the defendant in Brazil against the plaintiff. The defendant contended that by the Brazilian law libel was a crime, not a tort, for which he could be prosecuted at the instance of the plaintiff.

The Court of Appeal, speaking through Lopez, L.J., dismissed the plea of the defendant, holding thereby that the act of the defendant of publishing a libelous matter against the plaintiff in Brazil was not innocent and therefore not justifiable. Rigby, L.J., while agreeing with Lopez, L.J., added yet another dimension to the ratio employed by the latter, by asserting that the change of language from 'actionable' to 'justifiable' on the part of Willis J. in *Phillips v. Eyre* was deliberate.

It is a matter of pity that the learned judge in *Machado v. Fontes* failed to understand that Willis J. employed the word justifiable' for the act of indemnity passed by the local legislature of Jamaica, designed to exonerate the ex-governor of Jamaica for the wrong he committed of assaulting and falsely imprisoning the plaintiff during an emergency. The reviewer cannot withhold his lurking temptation to comment here, that when compared to the startling judgment in *Machado v. Fontes*, the judgment of the Rajasthan High Court in Kotah Transport Limited case, based on a literal interpretation of the twin criteria of Willis, J. in *Phillips v Eyre*, stands salvaged. Be that as it may.

Appropriately, therefore, the House of Lords in *Chaplin v. Boys, (1969) 2 ALL ER 1085* overruled by a majority the unfortunate decision in *Machado v. Fontes*. Lord Donovan in the said case of *Chaplin v. Boys* observed that the unfortunate decision in *Machado v. Fontes* is a clear case of 'blatant forum shopping'. No doubt the House of Lords could take credit for putting an end to the unhealthy practice of forum shopping in respect of foreign torts. Even so, it failed to carry its judgment to its logical conclusion by embracing the proper law of tort, comparable to the proper law of contract, of J.H.C. Morris which would help eliminate altogether the much maligned 'double actionability doctrine'. Inevitably, therefore, it required legislative intervention by the passing of an enactment by the British Parliament, namely, Private International Law (Miscellaneous Provisions), Act, 1995, subject to only one exception, namely, defamation (see Section 10 of the Act).

Part III-I

LAW OF PERSONS

Marriage and Matrimonial Causes

———

A case study of marriage and matrimonial causes in Conflict of Laws offers the reviewer ample scope for a critical appraisal. This is not the case with other areas of this subject, barring domicile, which, as commented upon earlier in Part I, is most nebulous and intriguing.

We have cases where courts in India have exercised jurisdiction and granted relief in marriages between petitioning husbands and foreign wives, even though they were church marriages, on the strength of the Special Marriage Act, 1954, which was given an all pervasive scope and effect or, as the case may be, on the basis of the outmoded concept that the domicile of the wife, on marriage, follows that of her husband.

Interestingly enough, we have cases where grant of *ex parte* decrees of divorce of husbands who fraudulently claim to have acquired domicile by a made-believe stay of three months or, as the case may be, six weeks as in the States of Nevada, Missouri, and New Mexico of the United States of America. Interestingly enough, we have a case of matrimonial adventure of an NRI who seeks and obtains an *ex parte* decree of divorce from his Indian wife though a court in the United States. The learned judge of the Supreme Court of India, who wrote the judgment in the case, recommended the passing of legislation by the Union of India incorporating three principles, the first of which runs thus: 'No marriage between a NRI and an Indian woman which has taken place in India may be annulled by a foreign court'.

The reviewer has constrained the remark how an Indian judge can dictate to the judge of a foreign court to refrain from exercising jurisdiction contrary to the basic rule of Conflict of Laws, that the exercise of jurisdiction by a court is based on the twin criteria of submission of the respondent to its jurisdiction and the effectiveness of such exercise by it.

The landmark decision of the Supreme Court of India in Shah Bano Begum's case laid down the principle that a Muslim wife, even as her counterpart in other religions, is equally eligible to seek and obtain maintenance from a magistrate under Sections 3 and 4 of the Muslim Women (Protection of Rights on Divorce Act, 1986), laid down the rule that as per Section 3 (1) (a) of the Act, a divorced Muslim wife is entitled to seek and obtain from her former husband a reasonable and fair provision and maintenance to be made and paid to her for life within the *iddat* period.

There are other cases, highlighted in the case study, which would arouse the curiosity of the reader and wet his appetite.

Christopher Andrew Neelakantan v. Mrs Anne Neelakantan, Respondent, AIR 1959, Rajasthan 133

This is a judgment of the Rajasthan High Court in Civil Miscellaneous First Appeal No. 90 of 1958, as against the judgment of the District Judge of Jodhpur, dated 2 December 1958.

The facts of the case, briefly stated, are as follows:

The appellant, Christopher Andrew Neelakantan, was a Wing Commander in the India Air Force stationed in Jodhpur, Rajasthan, where he had his domicile. He was married to the Respondent, Mrs Anne Neelakantan, in a church in England. The couple never lived together, as the respondent flatly refused to go over to India and join her husband in Jodhpur, despite entreaties made to her by her husband. Mr Neelkantan, thereupon, filed a divorce petition in the Court of the District Judge, Jodhpur, on the ground of desertion seeking dissolution of his marriage with the respondent. The learned district judge dismissed the petition summarily. His dismissal order was based on Section 31 of the Special Marriage Act, 1954, which forbade recourse to the said Section 31 of the said Act in view of their marriage taking place in a church in England, not within the local limits of Jodhpur, Rajasthan, nor did they live there at Jodhpur as husband and wife.

The court relied on the view held by Cheshire in this regard which runs thus: 'Thus, for instance, a husband or wife domiciled abroad is not permitted to institute a suit in England for dissolution of marriage, since divorce jurisdiction resides exclusively in the court of the domicil' (G.C. Cheshire, *Private International Law*, Fourth Edition, p. 103).

It is understandable, therefore, the Rajasthan High

Court had to rely on the view held by *Lord Penzance in Niboyet v. Niboyet (1878) 4 PD*, where the learned judge states that a suit can be instituted in a court of that country where the spouses are domiciled, if an act treated as a matrimonial offence is committed by either of the parties arising from their being married. It is the domiciliary status of the spouses that invests the court of domicile to exercise jurisdiction and, that too, based on the archaic doctrine that the domicile of the wife follows that of her husband, if the husband were to seek a dissolution of their marriage. Further, the Rajasthan High Court opined that desertion is a valid ground for seeking a dissolution of a marriage under the Special Marriage Act, 1954, which does not find a place in Section 10 of the Indian Divorce Act 1869 (No. IV of 1869). In the High Court's view the Special Marriage Act, 1954, is of all-embracing nature which one could gather from its preamble. It is interesting, in this connection, to reproduce verbatim as to how the Court portrays the nature and scope of the Act. It runs thus:

It may also be pointed out, in this connection, that the preamble to the Act shows that so far as divorce is concerned, the Act is all embracing and would govern the dissolution of all marriages irrespective of the consideration whether the marriage is of special form envisaged in the Act and whether it has been registered under the Act or not. In this view of the matter, I can see nothing in the Act of 1954 which could exclude the application thereof to the case of the petitioner, no matter that the provisions of the Act of 1869 in that respect are somewhat narrower (I.N. Modi, J., Para 14 of the judgment).

It is interesting, in this connection, to draw the readers' attention to the contrary view held by the Allahabad High Court in *Aulvin v. Singh v. Chandrawati, AIR 1974 All. 178.*

That was a case where a decree of divorce was sought of a marriage between two Christians domiciled in India. The marriage was solemnized under the Indian Christian Marriage Act, 1872. The Court, while dismissing the petition seeking a decree of divorce, refused to apply the Special Marriage Act, 1954, for the grant of a decree of divorce on the ground that since the marriage was solemnized under the Indian Christian Marriage Act, 1872, relief can be sought only under the Christian law, that is the Indian Divorce Act, 1869.

The reviewer respectfully submits that he withholds any more comment on Christopher Andrew Neelakantan's case, for it seems that the Allahabad High Court's judgment may be deemed *res ipsa loquitur* on the issue of the so-called all-embracing nature of the Special Marriage Act, 1954!

Sri Aulvin v. Singh, Petitioner v. Smt. Chandravati, Respondent, AIR 1974, Allahabad 278

This case is a sequel to *Christopher Andrew Neelakantan v. Smt. Anne Neelakantan, AIR 1959 Rajasthan 133*. As was observed in the last paragraph of Neelakantan's case, inasmuch as the marriage in the case *Aulvin Singh v. Chandrawati* was solemnized between two Indian Christians under the Indian Christian Marriage Act, 1872, relief could be sought only under the Indian Divorce Act, 1869, and certainly not under the Special Marriage Act, 1954, thus negativing the so-called all-embracing character of the Special Marriage Act, 1954. Because desertion as a ground for divorce does not find a place in the Indian Divorce Act, 1869, the Allahabad High Court in Aulvin

Singh's case had to dismiss the appeal. Had the Foreign Marriage Act, 1969, been in existence when Neelakantan's case was decided, the Court would have straight away applied the said Act, thus setting at naught the fallacious ratio of imparting to the Special Marriage Act, 1954, an all-embracing status.

The above preliminary observation would help us to appreciate the ruling in Aulvin Singh's case.

The material facts that gave rise to the appeal to the Allahabad High Court in this case are briefly as follows:

The Appellant-Petitioner Aulvin Singh presented this appeal before the Allahabad High Court from the decree of dismissal by the learned district judge of the district of Dehradun of his petition against his wife Chandrawati for divorce on the ground of desertion. The said petition was brought under Section 27 of the Special Marriage Act, 1954. The learned district judge dismissed the petition on the ground that the parties were Christians who got married in a Christian church under the Indian Christian Marriage Act (Act No. XV of 1872), and, as such, could seek a dissolution of the marriage only under Section 10 of the Indian Divorce Act (14 of 1869) and not under Section 27 of the Special Marriage Act, 1954, as they failed to get their marriage registered under Section 15 of the Act.

The Appellant-Petitioner Aulvin Singh alleged that his wife Chandrawati left her matrimonial home for no cause and joined her father, refusing to live with her husband any longer. She spurned her husband's entreaties to go back to him. Smt. Chandrawati, for her part, pleaded that she was beaten and ill-treated by her husband that forced her to leave her matrimonial home and seek refuge at her father's house. The learned district judge dismissed the petition holding thereby that it was not maintainable under Section 27 of the Special Marriage Act, 1954. As stated earlier, the petition could not be as one under Section 10 of the Divorce Act, 1869, as desertion is not a ground for dissolution of a marriage under the Act. The Allahabad High Court confirmed the lower court's judgment and dismissed the appeal for lacking merit.

Comment is superfluous. As observed earlier in the preliminary remarks, this judgment of the High Court of Allahabad is a death-blow to the ruling of the Rajasthan High Court in Neelakantan's case imparting to the Special Marriage Act, 1954, an all-embracing status.

John Jiban Chandra Datta v. Abinash Chandra Sen, 1939 ILR2 Calcutta 12

This case raises an interesting question under Conflict of Laws, namely whether a Christian husband domiciled in India can, on his conversion to Islam, validly take a second wife as under Mahomedan Law; and, further, whether he could divorce his Christian wife, also an Indian domiciliary, by pronouncing *talaq*. While the answer to the first part of the question is 'yes', for he has become a Muslim by embracing Islam, the answer to the second part of the question is an emphatic 'no', for the wife continues to be an Indian Christian and, as such, is governed by the Indian Divorce Act, 1869. The facts of the case, briefly stated, are as follows:

The appeal to the High Court of Calcutta arose out of a suit for declaration of title to and recovery of possession and partition of land mentioned in the plaint. It was admitted by both the parties that the land was originally owned by one Dukiram who professed the Christian faith. It was, however, alleged by the plaintiff that Dukhiram subsequently became a covert to Islam, married a woman of the name of Alfatanessa and had a daughter by her who figured as defendant No. 3 who conveyed to the plaintiff the land which she obtained by right of inheritance under the Mahomedan Law.

The learned Subordinate Judge, before whom the case was instituted, found that all three facts, namely, the conversion of Dukhiram from Christianity to Islam which made him a Mahomedan, his subsequent marriage to Alfatanessa, a Mahomedan, and the birth of defendant No. 3 born of Alfatanessa had all been proved. On appeal the learned district judge upheld all three findings of the learned subordinate judge.

Under Mahomedan Law, however, where a Christian who embraced Islam acquired all the rights which a Mahomedan is endowed with, and could contract a valid marriage even though the first one with the Christian wife subsists. If, on the contrary, the first marriage were contracted in England under English forms, during its subsistence the second marriage would be regarded as a nullity (see *R.V. Hammersmith Superintendent Registrar of Marriages, ex parte Mir Anwaruddin (1917) 1 K.B. 634*). In the present case, both the parties were domiciled in India and both the marriages of Dukhiram were solemnized here in India. Accordingly, the Calcutta High Court held that Dukhiram who embraced Islam and then entered into a second marriage with Alfatanessa could under Mahomedan Law validly do so, and that defendant No. 3, his daughter, who rightly inherited her share under the Mahomedan Law, which she conveyed to the plaintiff, was entitled to do so. Based on the above mentioned findings, the Court dismissed the appeal with costs.

The decision of the Calcutta High Court speaks for itself and, therefore, does not call for any comment.

Sarla Mudgal, President Kalyani and Ors. v. Union of India and Ors. 1995, AIR 1531, 1995 SCC (3) 635, JT 1995 (4) 331, 1995 Scale (3) 286

The issue that arose for consideration by the Supreme Court of India in Sarla Mudgal and other related cases is whether a Hindu husband who got married to a Hindu woman under the Hindu Marriage Act, 1955, which strictly professes monogamy, can by embracing Islam enter into a second marriage which, according to Section 494 of the Indian Penal Code (IPC) is bigamous and, as such, punishable. Under Islamic personal law a Muslim husband or an apostate to Islam can divorce his Muslim wife extra-judicially by pronouncing the word 'talaq' without having to assign any reason for it and marry, yet again, as many as four wives.

Four writ petitions were filed under Article 32 of the Constitution of India. Petitioner 1 was the President of 'Kalyani'—a registered Society—an organization working for the welfare of needy families and women in distress.

The ratio employed by Hon'ble Mr Justice Kuldip Singh in pronouncing a verdict that a Hindu husband who by embracing Islam married again a Muslim lady or a Hindu woman who, too, embraced Islam prior to her marriage to him is punishable for bigamy as per Sections 494 and 495 of the IPC leaves much to be desired.

The learned judge in coming to the conclusion set out above ratiocinates thus: '....it is no doubt correct that the marriage solemnized by a Hindu husband after embracing Islam may not be strictly a void marriage under the Act (namely the Hindu Marriage Act, 1955) because he is no longer a Hindu, *but the fact remains that the marriage would be in violation of the Act which strictly professes monogamy'.*

The first part of the reasoning is unquestionably valid on the basis of Section 11 as read with Section 5 (i), (iv), and (v) of the Hindu Marriage Act. On the contrary, the second part of the reasoning leaves much to be desired, inasmuch as the Hindu Marriage Act, 1955, which strictly professes monogamy has no longer any hold over the husband who ceases to be a Hindu after having embraced Islam.

The learned judge further elaborates in three paragraphs (page 9, para 3) that which he has adumbrated earlier in just five lines, set out above. It is as follows:

The expression 'void' for the purpose of the Act has been defined under Section 11 of the Act. It has a limited meaning within the scope of the definition under the section. On the other hand, the same expression has a different purpose under Section 494, IPC, and has to be given meaningful interpretation. The expression 'void' under Section 494, IPC has been used in the wider sense. A marriage which is in violation of any provision of law would be void in terms of the expression used under Section 494, IPC.

A Hindu marriage solemnized under the Act can only be dissolved on any of the grounds specified under the Act. Till the time a Hindu marriage is dissolved under the Act, none of the spouses can contract a second marriage. Conversion to Islam and marrying again would not, by itself, dissolve the Hindu marriage under the Act. *The second marriage by a convert would therefore be in violation of the Act and as such void in terms of Section 494, IPC. Any act which is in violation of mandatory provisions of law is per se void.*

The ratio employed by Hon'ble Mr Justice Kuldip Singh, set out above is, with due respect to him, specious. There is nothing like the second marriage solemnized by a Hindu husband, a convert to Islam, being not construed void under the Hindu Marriage Act, 1955, in the narrower sense and it being construed void in the wider sense in that the said second marriage runs counter to the Act *which strictly professes monogamy.*

Even conceding that the life of the law has not been logic, the Hindu Marriage Act, 1955, which strictly professes monogamy does not come for reckoning as against the Hindu husband who, after having embraced Islam, is governed by the Muslim personal law which permits polygamy.

The question whether Section 494 of the IPC which punishes polygamy overrides the Muslim personal law which permits polygamy. The answer to the above query is an emphatic 'no'. This view is further fortified by the dictum of the Privy Council in an early twentieth century case, namely, 'clear proof of usage outweighs the written text of the law'.

To override a custom or a usage there need be a subsequent enactment which expressly abrogates any custom or a usage to the contrary.

In this connection, we may draw the attention of the reader to the Parsi Marriage and Divorce Act, 1936, as amended in 1988, entitled The Parsi Marriage and Divorce (Amendment) Act, 1988. Sections 4 and 5 of the amended version are set out below:

Section 4 — Remarriage when Unlawful

(1) No Parsi (whether such Parsi has changed his or her religion or domicile or not) shall contract any marriage under this Act or any other law in the lifetime of his or her wife or husband, whether a Parsi or not, except after his or her lawful divorce from such wife or husband or after his or her marriage with such wife or husband has lawfully been declared null and void or dissolved,

and, if the marriage was contracted with such wife or husband under the Parsi Marriage and Divorce, 1865, (Rep. by this Act), or under this Act, except after a divorce declaration as aforesaid under either of the said Acts.

(2) Every marriage contracted contrary to the provisions of subsection (1) shall be void.

Section 5 – Punishment of Bigamy

Every Parsi who during the lifetime of his or her wife or husband, whether Parsi or not, contracts a marriage without having been lawfully divorced from such wife or husband or without his or her marriage with such wife or husband having legally been declared null and void or dissolved, shall be subject to the penalties provided in Sections 494 and 495 of the IPC (45 of 1860) for the offence of marrying again during the lifetime of a husband or wife.

On the contrary, the Hindu Marriage Act, 1955 (25 of 1955), remains the same these 60 years without undergoing any amendment as set out, in particular, under sub-section 2 of Section 5 of the Parsi Marriage and Divorce (Amendment) Act, 1988. That being the case, the Hindu Marriage Act, 1955, which strictly professes monogamy cannot have any sway over a Hindu husband who after having embraced Islam marries a second Muslim wife which is not bigamous under Muslim personal law and, as such, not punishable under Sections 494 and 495 of the IPC (45 of 1860).

If that be not done, namely, amending the Hindu Marriage Act, 1955, prohibiting altogether a second marriage by any change of religion on the part of the erring Hindu husband or wife, Sections 494 and 495 of the IPC imposing punishment for bigamy will be of no avail, the strictly monogamous character of a Hindu marriage under the Hindu Marriage Act, 1955, notwithstanding.

It is not that the existing Hindu Marriage Act, 1955, despite the failure of the legislature of suitably amending it with a view to eliminate altogether matrimonial adventures on the part of either of the spouses, leaves the Hindu wife remediless for the judiciary to have recourse to the norm of justice, equity, and good conscience as advocated by Lodge, J. in *Sayeeda Khatun v. M. Obadiah, 49CWN745* or, as for that, by the Privy Council in *Waghela Rajsanji v. Sheik Masluddin (1887) 141A89*. The Hindu wife can seek a dissolution of her Hindu marriage on the ground of desertion for a period of two years by her husband as under Section 13 (1) (ib) and follow it up by seeking maintenance before a magistrate under Section 125 of the Criminal Procedure Code on the strength of the Supreme Court's decision in *Mohammad Ahmed Khan v. Shah Bano Begum, AIR 1985 SC 945* and *Daniel Latifi and Another v. Union of India, 2001 7 Sec 740*.

Further, it may respectfully be submitted that the reliance placed by the Supreme Court in the case under review on the decision of the Bombay High Court, the judgment for which was written by Mr Justice M.C. Chagla, J., as he then was. It is a matter of surprise that a judge of the calibre of Mr Justice Chagla failed to refer to the Parsi Marriage and Divorce Act, 1936, which clearly and unequivocally rules out embracing by either of the spouses any other religion prior to a second marriage, unless he or she get the subsisting Parsi marriage declared null and void by the tribunal contemplated under the Act and get the marriage dissolved. The question does not arise of the Parsi wife embracing Islam and yet learn to live happily with her Parsi husband as Mr Justice Chagla opined, instead of her pleading that she could not as a Muslim continue to live with her Parsi husband. The learned judge ought to have dismissed the wife's petition *in limine* on the strength of the Parsi Marriage and Divorce Act, 1936, not, as he did, erroneously have recourse to the doctrine of equity, justice, and good conscience which calls for dismissal of her petition. Be that as it may.

It is not without significance that Mr Justice Kuldip Singh emphasizes the need to have a uniform civil code in compliance with the Directive Principle of the Constitution of India as embodied in Article 44 of the Constitution. It is well worth quoting the words of wisdom of Mr Justice Kuldip Singh in this regard. He writes as under:

It appears that even 41 years thereafter, (i.e., after the Hindu Code Bill was piloted in 1954 by Pandit Jawahar Lal Nehru) the Rulers of the day are not in a mood to retrieve Article 44 from the cold storage where it is lying since 1949. The Governments which have come and gone have so far failed to make any effort towards a 'uniform personal law for all Indians'.

The Supreme Court of India had expressed, as of here, the same sentiment in a few cases of the failure of successive governments to usher in a uniform civil code in compliance with constitutional mandate embodied in Article 44, Part IV, of the Constitution under the heading The Directive Principles of State Policy which are non-justifiable.

We may here draw the attention of the readers to Article 21 of the Constitution of India under Part III of the Constitution, namely, Fundamental Rights, wherein it is stated that no person shall be deprived of his life or personal liberty except according to the procedure established by law. Right to livelihood, according to an earlier decision of the Supreme Court, is an integral facet of the right to life (see *Narendra Kumar v. State of Haryana, JT (1994) 2SC94*).

As the saying goes, *ubi jus ibi remedium* (where there is right there is remedy), the abandoned Hindu wife, who, in just assertion of her fundamental right to livelihood can seek a dissolution of her marriage under the Hindu Marriage Act, 1955, and follow it up by seeking maintenance for life. Of course, she will forfeit her separate residence and maintenance if she is unchaste or ceases to be a Hindu, as laid down in sub-section (3) of Section 18 of the Hindu Adoptions and Maintenance Act, 1956.

Where there is a fundamental right to livelihood inferable from Article 21 of the Constitution of India, we don't need to bemoan the failure of successive governments to usher in a 'unified personal law for all Indians'.

Before we talk of attempts to usher in a uniform civil code as ordained in Article 44 of the Constitution of India, we will do well to strive to integrate all our religious and ethnic minorities, instilling in them a sense of belonging to the nation. For so doing, it is incumbent on the overwhelming Hindu community to stretch its hand of friendship and comradery to all the religious and ethnic minority communities inhabiting our great nation with the avowed objective of assimilating them into the fabric of our society. To achieve such a laudable objective, politics and thoughtless past prejudices should be done away with once and for all.

Mr Justice R.N. Sahai in his concurring opinion draws our attention to the success of some of the predominantly Muslim States like Algeria, which escaped his attention, beside Syria, Tunisia, Morocco, Pakistan, Iran, the Islamic Republic of the former Soviet Union have codified their personal laws and have either done away with or severely restricted the baneful practice of polygamy. So he, too, advocates a unified civil code in keeping with our national ethos which is reflected in the constitutionally amended

version of the Preamble, namely, to ushering in a Sovereign
Socialist Secular Democratic Republic (see Constitution
Forty-Second Amendment Act, 1976). As pointed out
above, any talk of ushering in a common civil code in the
present scenario is nothing short of putting the cart before
the horse. To achieve the said objective, we should keep our
present day politicians at arm's length and set in motion
a movement with the avowed objective of integrating our
manifold religious and ethnic communities. We need to,
therefore, entrust the destiny of our nation to the rising
tide of motivated youths. The outcome of it all will not
only witness the emergence of an integrated great nation
and, as a natural concomitant, of ushering in a uniform
civil code will become a reality.

Sir Henry Sumner Maine in his work 'Ancient Law'
aptly remarks that 'the movement of the progressive
societies has hitherto been a movement from status to
contract'. Our Indian polity has to undergo a sea change, as
set out above, for our nation to deserve the nomenclature,
'a progressive society'.[1]

Satya v. Teja Singh, 1975 AIR 105; 1975 SCR (2) 97; 1975 SCC(I) 120

Abandonment of lawfully wedded wives by husbands
who go overseas either for higher studies or in search of
a lucrative profession or business is rampant in the State
of Punjab in the North and in the State of Kerala in the
South. The States of Nevada, New Mexico, in the United
States bestow domiciliary status for the mere asking by the
concerned by a so-called residence on his part of six or, as

[1] Sir Henry Sumner Maine, *Ancient Law* (London: George
Routledge and Sons Limited, 1913), pp. 417–18.

the case may be, twelve weeks. Surely the conferment of domiciliary status on a person on a make-belief residence in the said States for acquisition of domicile is nothing short of a mockery of the legal requirement in Conflict of Laws of *animo* et *facto* for such acquisition.

The case under review is one such. The respondent Teja Singh and the appellant Satya were Indian nationals and domiciliaries. They were married in Jullunder in the year 1959. Very soon after the marriage the respondent Teja Singh left for the United States for higher studies in forestry. For a year he studied in New York University. He, then, switched over to Utah for his doctoral programme in forestry and obtained a doctorate in the year 1964. From there he moved to Alberta, Canada, in the year 1965 and had taken up a job in the Department of Forestry, Alberta, Canada.

The State of Nevada which, as aforesaid, confers domiciliary status on a person by a mere six weeks stay there served his nefarious intent admirably of getting rid of his wife by obtaining a divorce from a court in the State of Nevada.

Mr Justice Chandrachud (as he then was) who wrote the judgment in this case aptly remarks that the respondent Teja Singh went to Nevada forum-hunting, found a convenient jurisdiction which would easily purvey a divorce to him and left it even before the ink on his domciliary assertion was dry. Accordingly, he concludes that the decree of the Nevada Court lacked jurisdiction and that, therefore, it does not warrant recognition by courts in India.

As a counter to the assertion of the respondent Teja Singh that the appellant Satya had ceased to be his wife by virtue of the decree of dissolution of the court in the State of Nevada and, accordingly, forfeited her right to be maintained by him, albeit his willingness to maintain her children, Satya petitioned to the judicial magistrate at Jullundur in the State of Punjab for maintenance. The learned magistrate allowed the maintenance petition of the appellant, holding thereby that the decree of divorce of the Court in Nevada, based on the make-believe domiciliary status of the respondent, was unacceptable and that the marriage between them could be dissolved only under the Hindu Marriage Act, 1955. On a revision petition filed by the respondent before the High Court of Punjab and Haryana, the learned single judge of that court allowed his petition, upholding thereby the decree of dissolution of the Court at Nevada, based on his acquisition of domicile there which automatically got extended to his appellant wife on the strength of the outmoded and archaic ruling of the Privy Council in *Le Mesurier v. Le Mesurier*, Attoney General for *Alberta v. Cook*, and of the House of Lords in England in *Lord Adovcate v. Jaffray*.

The Supreme Court, speaking through Mr Justice Chandrachud (as he then was), characterized the Nevada court's ruling a *brutum fulmen* based on the respondent's fraudulent assertion that he was domiciled there. It is, therefore, appropriate to pronounce a verdict that the court at Nevada by its ruling based on the so-called jurisdictional facts, was not just 'mistaken' but 'misled' by fraud and trickery played by the respondent. 'Fraud' in the words of Mr Justice De Grey in the Duchess of Kingston's case (1776), Harg. State Trials, 602, 'is an extrinsic, collateral act, violating all proceedings, even those of courts of justice'.

While allowing the appeal with costs, thereby setting aside the judgment of the High Court and restoring that of the trial court, Mr Justice Chandrachud made the following significant observation:

Our legislature ought to find a solution to such schizoid situations as the British Parliament has, to a large extent, done by passing the

'Recognition of Divorce and Legal Separations Act, 1971'. Perhaps, the International Hague Convention of 1970 which contains a comprehensive scheme for relieving the confusion caused by differing systems of Conflict of Laws may serve as a model. But any such law shall have to provide for the non-recognition of foreign decrees procured by fraud bearing on jurisdictional facts as also for the non-recognition of decrees, the recognition of which would be contrary to our public policy. Until then the courts shall have to exercise a residual discretion to avoid flagrant injustice; for, no rule of private international law could compel a wife to submit to a decree procured by the husband by trickery. Such decrees offend against our notion of substantial justice.

While commending the judgment of Mr Justice Chandrachud in this case, the first of its kind in matrimonial disputes, for its articulate ratiocination, the reviewer in all fairness to the task he has undertaken cannot but highlight certain deficiencies that cannot be overlooked. The learned judge would have acquitted himself more creditably, had he adopted a strictly issue-based approach to resolving the dispute. The two main issues that the Court was called upon to decide are: (i) whether the decree of divorce granted by the Court at Nevada, based on the acquisition by the respondent husband of a make-believe domicile that automatically communicated to the petitioning wife, ignoring the Hindu Marriage Act, 1955, altogether which was the governing law for the grant of a decree of divorce; and (ii) whether the Court at Nevada which granted an *ex parte* decree of divorce in conformity with its own procedural law for acquisition of domicile, ignoring, as aforesaid, the Hindu Marriage Act, 1955, for rendering justice to the case, was imposed upon by the respondent by his fraudulent assertion that he intended to make Nevada his permanent home which Section 13, sub-section (e) of the Civil Procedure Code, 1908, explicitly forbids.

Had only the learned Mr Justice Chandrachud confined himself to the two issues that called for a judicial determination, it undoubtedly would have been a classic judgment. One wonders, therefore, what prompted the learned judge to indulge in writing a dissertation on matrimonial law in Conflict of Laws, citing judicial decisions and juristic opinions, predominantly English!

Y. Narasimha Rao and ORS v. Y. Venkata Lakshmi and ANR, 1991 SCR (2) 821; 1991 SCC (3) 45

Facts

This case, principle-wise, is almost similar to Satya v. Teja Singh, though differing from it on certain vital aspects which make the judgment more interesting. Those, briefly stated, are as follows:

The respondent wife had in this case the means to contest her case in the United States by filing suitable replies to her husband's petition for dissolution of their marriage filed by him before the circuit court of St Louis in the State of Missouri. She could, besides, file a petition for bigamy against her husband, the first appellant, and his second wife, the second appellant, before a magistrate in the State of Andhra Pradesh which was discharged by the learned magistrate for her failure to make out a *prima facie* case against the appellants. She further contested the decision of the learned magistrate by filing a criminal revision petition before the High Court which mistakenly set aside the magisterial order of discharge by holding that a photostat copy of the dissolution of the marriage by the circuit court of St Louis, Missouri, based on which the learned magistrate made the said order, was inadmissible in evidence. In fact, the inadmissibility of the photostat copy of the decree of dissolution of the marriage by the circuit Court of Missouri arose out of non-compliance of the requirement of Section 86 of the Indian Evidence Act. That it should have also been certified by the representative of the Central Government in India, besides it being authenticated by the deputy clerk of the Circuit Court of Missouri, as per the requirement of Section 86 of the Indian Evidence Act. The dispute was taken up by the Supreme Court for adjudication by grant of special leave.

As in *Satya v. Teja Singh*, in this case, too, the appellant took up residence at St Louis, Missourie, for a period of 90 days as per the requirement of law of the State of Missouri for his acquiring domiciliary status to enable him to file a petition for a dissolution of his marriage with the respondent.

The respondent's marital stay with the appellant in the State of Andhra Pradesh was just for a period of four or five months before she left for her parental house at Relangi, West Godawari. The appellant, for his part, left for the United States seeking a placement in the medical service with the help of his friend Prasad, and obtained employment in Chicago in the first instance and, thereafter, in oak Forest and Greenville Springs and, ultimately, in the Charity Hospital in Louisiana at New Orleans where he continued to be employed.

In the petition filed by the appellant husband before the Circuit Court at St Louis, Missourie, he alleged that his wife joined him in New Orleans and they stayed together as husband and wife for a brief period before she left New Orleans for Jackson, Texas, in the first instance, and, thereafter, to Chicago for a brief stay with the petitioner's friend Prasad before finally leaving for India.

From the foregoing, it is obvious that the respondent never resided with the appellant at St Louis, Missouri, before she left the United States for India. The appellant in his petition filed before the Circuit Court at St. Louis, Missouri, averred that they ceased to live together as husband and wife for over a period of one year and that, therefore, their marriage should be deemed to have broken down irretrievably that called for a dissolution of their marriage.

The respondent wife filed two replies, almost similar, by which she asserted that she was totally unaware of the petitioner's so-called stay at St Louis for a period of 90 days prior to his seeking dissolution of their marriage. Besides, she categorically questioned the jurisdiction of St Louis Circuit Court to entertain the petition.

As in *Satya v. Teja Singh* case, the Circuit Court at St Louis was misled, certainly not mistaken, as to its jurisdiction sought by the fraudulent husband, a mere bird of passage, which, undoubtedly, vitiated the solemn proceedings of the Circuit Court.

While dismissing the appeal preferred by the husband, Y. Narasimha Rao, the Supreme Court, speaking through Mr Justice Sawant, made the following significant observation:

Since with regard to the jurisdiction of the forum as well as the ground on which it is passed the foreign decree in the present case is not in accordance with the Act under which the parties were married and the respondent had not submitted to the jurisdiction of the court or consented to the passing, it cannot be recognized by the courts in this country and is, therefore, unenforceable (see para 14 of the judgment).

It is respectfully submitted that the exercise of jurisdiction by a municipal court in a conflicts case, being a procedural matter, is for the *lex fori* to determine in conformity with its rules of conflict of laws. On the contrary, the grant of relief which, indubitably, is a matter of substance, calls for the application of the law of the country where the marriage took place, namely the Hindu Marriage Act, 1955.

We are constrained to bring to the notice of the Supreme Court that a foreign judgment, as per the rules of Conflict of Laws, does not become final and binding until and unless the decree of divorce granted by the foreign court is brought before the designated Indian court by the errant husband for recognition and enforcement.

In this case under review the decree of divorce granted by the Circuit Court at St Louis, Missourie, suffers from two major infirmities. Firstly, it gives a go-by to the basic norm of judicial dispensation, namely, *audi alteram partem*, that is, hear the other party, in that the decree is *ex parte*. Secondly, the grant of substantive relief, namely, the issuance of a decree of dissolution of the Hindu marriage by the Circuit Court at St Louis ought to be, as per rules of conflict of laws, based on appropriate ground of the Hindu Marriage Act, 1955. The ground based on which the decree of dissolution of the Hindu marriage was granted by Circuit Court of St Louis, namely, irretrievable breakdown of the marriage, does not find a place in the Hindu Marriage Act, 1955.

As pointed out earlier, the Supreme Court, speaking through Mr Justice Sawant, employed a ratio that is *ex facie* out of tune with the law to be applied by a municipal court in the conflict resolution process. It is a basic rule of conflict of laws that in matters of procedure like exercise of jurisdiction, a municipal court is bound by its own *lex fori*. On the contrary, on issues relating to grant of substantive relief, such as passing of a decree of dissolution of a marriage as is the case under review, the court is bound to apply the matrimonial law of India, namely the Hindu Marriage Act, 1955, which is the *lex causæ*.

In the considered opinion of the reviewer, there is a mix up in the ratio employed by the learned judge in respect of the law to govern matters of procedure like exercise of jurisdiction, that can only be the *lex fori*. On the contrary, on issues relating to the grant of substantive relief such as decreeing dissolution of the marriage can be none other than the *lex causæ*.

However, a foreign judgment does not automatically become binding on the parties, unless it be endorsed by the court where the cause of action arose, which calls for the application of the *lex causæ*, that is, the Hindu Marriage Act, 1955. The said court is free to examine the foreign judgment for its due compliance with not only the substantive law of the country, namely, the Hindu Marriage Act, 1955, but also the country's procedural law, such as Section 13 of the Civil Procedure Code, 1908. The conclusiveness of the foreign judgment and even the exercise of jurisdiction by the foreign court lend themselves for scrutiny by the Indian court for its due compliance with not only the relevant ground of the Hindu Marriage Act, 1955, but also with certain vital procedural norms enshrined in Section 13 of the Indian Civil Procedure Code, such as sub-sections (c), (e), and (f).[2] These procedural

[2] Sub-section (c): Where it, namely the conclusiveness of the foreign judgment, appears on the face of the proceedings to be founded on an incorrect view of international law or a refusal to recognize the law of India in the case in which such law is applicable; Sub-section (e): where it has been obtained by fraud; Sub-section (f): where it sustains a claim founded on a breach of any law in force in India.

norms are as vital as the substantive law (that is, the Hindu Marriage Act, 1955) for a due determination by the foreign court of the matrimonial dispute.

Once the Indian court endorses a foreign judgment for its due compliance with not only the relevant ground of the Hindu Marriage Act, 1955, but also with the said procedural norms of Section 13 of the Indian Civil Procedure Code, the foreign judgment secures its finality and decisiveness for its due execution by the Indian court.

Neeraja Saraph v. Jayant Saraph, 1994 SCC (6) 461

This case is yet another NRI matrimonial adventure. For the respondent Jayant Saraph it was a pleasure trip to India which served as well to assuage the sentiments of his parents, by taking an Indian bride. For the victim Neeraja Saraph it was 'loss of everything, her maidenhood, status, service, dignity and peace'.

The above description speaks for itself and, therefore, serves the reviewer of recourse to any detailed narration of the story that led to the ruination of the cherished values of life that the appellant might have dreamed of prior to her marriage with the respondent.

Stated briefly, the first respondent, a computer hardware engineer, accomplished with a doctoral degree from the United States that earned him an employment there, visited India at the behest of his father to get married to the appellant in the first week of August 1989, and, soon thereafter, he took his wife for a honeymoon to Goa. He returned to the United States in the fourth week of August, 1989, never to look back again, unmindful of the pain and agony caused to his deserted wife. He wrote to the appellant thrice, all within three months, persuading her to give up her lucrative job which made her life comfortable. Trusting her villainous husband, she earnestly tried for a visa and even gave up her job in the month of November, 1989. In January 1990, the appellant's father wrote a letter to his untrustworthy son-in-law, narrating to him the untold sufferings of his daughter which failed to fetch any favourable response. As irony would have it, the respondent Jayant Saraph sent through his brother two envelops to be handed over to the appellant, one a petition for annulment of his marriage in a USA court and another a letter from her father-in-law pretending to be sympathetic to her plight which, from her father-in-law's standpoint, appeared to be honest and heartfelt.

The forlorn Neeraja Saraph filed a suit before a local court for damages *in forma pauperis* against her husband, the first appellant before the Supreme Court, and her father-in-law the second appellant before the Court. The suit was decreed *ex parte* for a sum of 22 lakhs and odd. On an appeal filed by the respondent against the said decree of the lower court, the High Court initially made an interim order, after staying operation of the *ex parte* decree of, the lower court by which the appellant's father-in-law, the second appellant before the Supreme Court was required to deposit a sum of Rs 1,00,000 within a month of the date of the order. The said order permitted the appellant to withdraw 50 per cent of it. The High Court, subsequently, modified its earlier order by which the second appellant was required to deposit Rs 3,00,000, including Rs 1,00,000, within a period of two months from the date of the order as a condition precedent to staying the execution of the *ex parte* decree of the lower court. The appellant was permitted to withdraw Rs 1,00,000 without any security, the remaining Rs 2,00,000 to be deposited in a nationalized bank as fixed deposit, the accruing interest on the said deposit to be paid to the appellant every month. Further, if the proceedings relating to *ex parte* decree dragged on beyond what would be deemed a reasonable period, the appellant would well be within her right to move an application for the withdrawal of further amount.

The learned Mr Justice R.M. Sahai deprecated the concept of domicile, as interpreted and applied by courts as opposed to the concept of nationality, as elusive leading to results which defy logic and rationality. If by a whimsical reading of the concept of *animo et facto* for acquisition of domicile of choice, courts may deny a person a domicile of a country where he resided for life, as in cases like *Winans v. A.G.*[3] and *Ramsay v. Liverpool Royal Infirmary*[4] equally astounding cases like re O' Keefe[5] where domicile is foisted on a person in a country by the court's recourse to the so-called concept of domicile of origin, which is neither the country of birth nor of residence for life of the concerned. Justifiably, we are constrained to remark 'enough is enough' with the so-called concept of domicile.

In the light of the foregoing, in the considered opinion of the reviewer, the concept of 'habitual residence' as the determinant of domicile, fortified by a United Nations Convention, take precedence. Be that as it may.

The learned Mr Justice R.M. Sahai would advocate enactment by the Union of India of legislation akin to the Foreign Judgment (Reciprocal Enforcement) Act, 1933, of the British Parliament. On the top of it all, with a view to safeguarding the interest of the Indian women from the

[3] 1904 A.C. 187.

[4] (1930) A.C. 588.

[5] (1940) Ch. 124.

clutches of heartless non-resident Indian husbands, he would urge the passing of a legislation by the Union of India, incorporating provisions such as:

(1) No marriage between a NRI and an Indian woman which has taken place in India may be annulled by a foreign court.
(2) Provision may be made for adequate alimony to the wife in the property of the husband both in India and abroad.
(3) The decree granted by Indian courts may be made executable in foreign courts both on principle of comity and by entering into reciprocal agreements like Section 44-A of the Civil Procedure Code which makes foreign decree executable as it would have been a decree passed by that court.

The above recommendation of the learned judge addressed to the legislature, designed to safeguarding the interests of Indian women, is pivotal to the ratio employed by him. While one would unhesitatingly endorse the second and the third recommendations as wholesome and efficacious in serving the interests of the hapless Indian wives of non-resident Indian husbands, the same is not the case with the first recommendation. It, in fact, is not only out of tune with the basic tenets of the science of Conflict of Laws governing assumption of jurisdiction by a foreign court, but virtually strikes at the very root of the doctrine of comity which, interestingly enough, receives endorsement in his own third recommendation. The learned judge is not unaware of the rule of conflict of laws that a foreign judgment is not credited with finality and conclusiveness unless it is approved and accepted by a designated court where the cause of action arose.

Mohd. Ahmed Khan, Petitioner v. Shah Bano Begum and Others, Respondents, AIR 1985 SC 945

This is a landmark decision of the Supreme Court. A Bench consisting of five eminent judges unequivocally declared that Section 125 of the Code of Criminal Procedure, 1898, is truly secular in character. In fact, Clause (b) of the Explanation to Section 125 (1), which defines 'wife' so as to include a divorced wife, does not contain any words of limitation whatsoever to justify the exclusion of Muslim women from its scope and ambit.

Mr Justice Chandrachud (C.J.), writing the judgment for the Bench, sought the weighty opinion of Sir James Fitzjames Stephen who piloted the Code of Criminal Procedure, 1872, as a Legal Member of the Viceory's Council, described the precursor of Chapter IX of the Code in which Section 125 figures, as 'a mode of preventing vagrancy' or 'at least of preventing its consequence'. The learned judge cites two earlier decisions of the Supreme Court to fortify his considered view as to the secular character of Section 125 of the Code of Criminal Procedure, 1973, which invests a First Class magistrate with jurisdiction to issue a maintenance order against a callous husband who, despite having sufficient means, refuses to maintain his discarded wife who has no means of her own to keep her body and soul together. Here the articulation may sound a bit rhetorical, but it brings home tellingly the scope and effect of Section 125 of the Code of Criminal Procedure.

In *Jagir Kaur v. Jaswant Singh*,[6] Subba Rao, J., speaking for the Court, said that Chapter XXXVI of the Code of 1898

---

[6] 1964 (2) SCR 73, 84.

which contains Section 488, corresponding to Section 125, 'intends to serve a social purpose'. In *Nanak Chand v. Shri Chandra Kishore Agarwala*,[7] Sikri, J., while pointing out that the scope and effect of the Hindu Adoptions and Maintenance Act, 1956, and that of Section 488 was different, said that Section 488 was 'applicable to all persons belonging to all religions and has no relationships with the personal law of the parties'.

The wife's right to maintenance under Section 488 of the Code of Criminal procedure, in the Court's view, depended upon the continuance of her married status. The said right could be defeated by the husband by divorcing her unilaterally by pronouncing *talaq* under the Muslim Personal law or, as the case may be, by obtaining a decree of divorce under the other systems of law. Therefore, with a view to eliminate the hardship caused to a divorced wife, the Joint Committee recommended that the benefit of the provisions relating to maintenance should be extended to a divorced woman so long as she has not remarried after her getting divorced. That, in the court's view, is the genesis of the Explanation to Section 125 (1) of the Cr. P.C., which provides that 'wife' includes a woman who has been divorced by the husband as also a woman who has obtained a divorce from her husband and has not remarried. Even in the absence of the provision, the courts had held that under the Code of 1898 the provisions regarding maintenance were independent of the personal law governing the parties. Accordingly, the induction of the definition of a 'wife' so as to include a divorced woman lends even greater weight to that conclusion.

[7] 1970 (1) SCR 565.

As has been made abundantly clear, the epithet 'wife' for the purpose of grant of maintenance by a first class magistrate is secular and, if we may say so, blind to religion. So much so, a Muslim woman, even as her counterpart in other religions, is equally eligible to seek and obtain maintenance from a magistrate under Section 125 provided, of course, she has not re-married.

The learned judge, in the course of the judgment, falls back upon the Privy Council's enunciation of the nature and character of *mahr* or dower, specified or unspecified at the time of the Muslim marriage, in the case *Hamira Bibi v. Zubaide Bibi*[8] an appeal from the Full Bench decision of the Allahabad High Court.

The Privy Council holds the view that dower is in consideration for the marriage and, as such, in theory it is payable before consummation; but the law allows its division into two parts, namely, prompt dower, payable before the wife can be called upon to enter the conjugal domicil and the other deferred dower, payable on the dissolution of the contract by the death of the parties or by divorce.[9]

Placing reliance on the statement of law in the instant case by Syed Ameer Ali who was a party to this decision and that of Sir Shadi Lal in yet another Privy Council's decision in the case *Sabir Hussain v. Farzand Hasan*,[10] the Court infers that the payment of dower may be deferred to a future date as, for example, death or divorce. But that does not, in the court's view, mean that the payment of the dower is occasioned by these events.

---

[8] 43 1.A.294, 864.
[9] pp. 300–1.
[10] 65 1.A.119, 127.

Mr Justice Chandrchud, C.J. yet again moots the issue of the desirability of ushering in a uniform civil code as ordained in Article 44 of the Constitution of India, which is one of the Directive Principles enshrined in Part IV of the Constitution, though non-justiciable as contrasted with Fundamental Rights of Part III which are judicially enforceable.

In this connection, the learned judge draws our attention to the persuasive view held by Professor Tahir Mahmood, an esteemed colleague of the learned judge, as highlighted in his book, entitled 'Muslim Personal Law' (1977 Edition, pp. 200–2). Therein he advocates the need to usher in a uniform civil code for all the citizens of India in faithful compliance with the Directive Principle embodied in Article 44 of the Constitution of India. He stigmatizes the State for its lack of will to do it in these words: 'In pursuance of the goal of secularism, the State must stop administering religion based on personal laws'. In this connection, he suggests that the lead should come from the majority community. However, the State should act to fulfil its mission of ushering a uniform civil code whether the lead expected of the majority community is forthcoming or not. In this connection, he makes a fervent appeal to the Muslim community in these words: 'Instead of wasting their energies in exerting theological and political pressure in order to secure an 'immunity' for their traditional personal law from the State legislative jurisdiction, the Muslim will do well to begin exploring and demonstrating how the true Islamic laws, purged of their time-worn and anachronistic interpretations, can enrich the common civil code of India'.

Mr Justice Chandrachud also adverts to the view expressed by Professor Tahir Mahmood at a seminar held on 18 October 1980, under the auspices of the Department of Islamic and Comparative Law, Indian Institute of Islamic Studies, New Delhi. He, yet again, made an appeal to the Muslim community to display by their conduct a correct understanding of Islamic concepts on marriage and divorce.

Appropriately enough, the learned judge draws our attention to the Report of the Commission on Marriage and Family Laws, that was appointed by the Government of Pakistan by a Resolution dated 4 August 1955. The answer of the Commission to question No. 5 (page 1215 of the Report) is that 'as a large number of middle-aged women who are being divorced without rhyme or reason should not be thrown on the streets without a roof over their heads and without any means of sustaining themselves and their children'. The Report concludes: 'In the words of Allama Iqbal', 'the question which is likely to confront Muslim countries in the near future, is whether the law of Islam is capable of evolution—a question which will require great intellectual effort, and is sure to be answered in the affirmative'.

The Court, while dismissing the appeal as highlighted by Mr Justice Chandrachud, admitted that seemingly insuperable difficulties are involved in bringing persons of different faiths and persuasions on a common platform. All the same, he averred that a beginning is to be made if the Constitution is to have any meaning. In that case, the role of the reformer is to be assumed by the courts because, as he justifiably remarks, that 'it is beyond the endurance of sensitive minds to allow injustices to be suffered when it is so palpable'. He, nevertheless, concedes that piecemeal attempts of courts to bridge the gap between personal laws cannot take the place of a common Civil Code for the obvious reason that justice to all is a far more satisfactory way of dispensing justice than justice from case to case.

This observation of Mr Justice Chandrachud reminds us of the caveat sounded by Lord Wilberforce in *Chaplin v. Boys*, 1969, 2 All E.R. 1085,[11] a case on foreign torts, when he observed by way of criticism of the American 'centre of gravity' or 'grouping of contacts' rule in preference to a traditional doctrinaire approach to resolving conflicts, that 'case-to-case decisions do not add up to a system of justice'.[12]

By way of concluding remarks, the reviewer re-iterates the observation that he made in Sarla Mudgal's case, namely that 'when there is a fundamental right to livelihood inferable from Article 21 of the Constitution of India,[13] we don't need to bemoan the failure of successive governments to usher in a 'unified personal law for all Indians'.

Danial Latifi and Another v. Union of India (2001) 7 SCC 740

This was a writ petition filed under Article 32 of the Constitution of India, challenging the validity of the Muslim Women (Protection of Rights on Divorce) Act, 1986, as violative of the Fundamental Rights guaranteed under Articles 14, 15, and 21 of the Constitution.

This judgment is, indeed, an endorsement of the ruling in Shah Bano Begum by the Supreme Court, namely, that the husband's liability towards his divorced Muslim wife does not cease, as per Muslim Personal Law, with the expiration of the period of iddat, but extends beyond in view of Section 125 of the Code of Criminal Procedure, 1973, which authorizes a divorced wife, irrespective of religion,

[11] [1969] 2 All. E.R. 1085.

[12] At p. 1104.

[13] See *Narendra Kumar v. State of Haryana, JT (1994) 2 SC 94.*

to seek and obtain maintenance, if she be not in a position to maintain herself after the period of iddat provided, of course, she does not contract a second marriage. The judgment in the case under review is directed to examine the constitutional validity of Sections 3 and 4 of the Muslim Women (Protection of Rights on Divorce) Act, 1986, an enactment passed by the Union Parliament as a sequel to the ruling of the Supreme Court in Shah Bano Begum's case.

Section 3 of the Act is vital to a divorced wife in that it vests in her a right to obtain from the former husband maintenance, provision, and mahr, as also to recover from his possession her wedding presents and dowry through the instrumentality of a magistrate who is authorized to order payment or restoration of these sums or properties. More importantly, Section 3 (1) (a) of the Act entitles a divorced wife to seek and obtain from her former husband a reasonable and fair provision and maintenance to be made and paid to her within the iddat period. The husband has a two-fold obligation under the said provision, namely (1) to make a reasonable and a fair provision for his divorced wife; and (2) to provide maintenance for her, all within the iddat period.

Contradicting the contention put forth on behalf of the Union of India that a divorced Muslim woman who is entitled to *mata* or maintenance is only a single or one time transaction which does not mean payment of maintenance continuously at all. The court speaking through Mr Justice Rajendra Babu made the following observation:

'This contention apart from supporting the view that the word provision in Section 3 (1) (a) of the Act incorporates mata as a right of a divorced Muslim woman distinct from and in addition to mahr and maintenance for the iddat period, also enables a reasonable and fair provision as provided under Section 3 (3) of the Act would be with reference to the needs of the divorced woman, the means of the husband, and the standard of life the woman enjoyed during the marriage, and there is no reason why such a provision could not take the form of the regular payment of alimony to the divorced woman, though it may look ironical that the enactment intended to reverse the decision in Shah Bano case, actually codifies the very rationale contained therein'.

While upholding the validity of the Act, the Court sums up its conclusion as follows:

(1) A Muslim husband is liable to make a reasonable and fair provision for the future of the divorced wife which obviously includes her maintenance as well. Such a reasonable and fair provision extends beyond the iddat period in terms of Section 3 (1) (a) of the Act.
(2) Liability of a Muslim husband to his divorced wife arising under Section 3 (1) (a) of the Act to pay maintenance is not confined to the iddat period.
(3) A divorced Muslim woman who has not remarried and who is not able to maintain herself after iddat period can proceed under Section 4 of the Act against her relatives who are liable to maintain her in proportion to the properties which they inherit on her death, according to Muslim law, from such divorced woman including her children and parents. If any of the relatives being unable to pay maintenance, the magistrate may direct the State Wakf Board established under the Act to pay such maintenance.
(4) The provisions of the Act do not offend Articles 14, 15, and 21 of the Constitution of India.

The judgment in this case, in the estimate of the reviewer, is logical, coherent, and pragmatic. It is no exaggeration to say that this ruling, while endorsing the epoch-making judgment in Shah Bano case, is, in fact, a trendsetter for the future in respect of the rights and claims of a divorced Muslim woman against her former husband.

Munavvar-ul-Islam (Appellant) v. Rishu Arora @ Rukhsar, Respondent. 9 May 2014

This was a case where a Muslim wife by name Rishu Arora @ Rukhsar who got converted to Hinduism, which was her original religious fold prior to her conversion to Islam and her marriage to the appellant Muanvvar-ul-Islam, obtained a decree of divorce from the trial court. On an appeal filed by the Muslim husband to the Delhi High Court, a Division Bench headed by Mr Justice Ravindra Bhat and Mr Justice Najmi Waziri, speaking through Mr Justice Najmi Waziri upholding the decree of divorce of the trial court in favour of the respondent Muslim wife, made the following significant observation:

In the light of the above discussion, and the admitted fact that the Respondent was originally a Hindu, who converted to her original faith from Islam, this Court holds that she falls within the second *proviso* to Section 4 of the Act (namely the Dissolution of Muslim Marriage Act, 1939) which is properly described as an exception to the Section. Her marriage is accordingly regulated not by the rule enunciated in Section 4, rather by the pre-existing Muslim personal law, which dissolves marriage upon apostasy *ipso facto*.

In this connection, we may recall the ruling in *Sayeeda Khatun v. M. Obadiah*[14] where a Jewish wife embraced Islam and then petitioned the court for a declaration that her Jewish marriage had been dissolved. The Court speaking through Lodge, J. made the observation, 'The plaintiff (the converting wife) has since converted to Islam and may in some respects be governed by the Mahomedan law....... I can find no authority for the view that a

[14] 49 CWN 745.

marriage solemnized according to one personal law can be dissolved according to another law simply because one of the two parties has changed his/her religion'. Accordingly, Lodge, J. had to lean on the norm of justice, equity, and good conscience in deciding the case which resulted in the dismissal of the petition.

Chagla, J. in the case *Robasa Khanum v. Khodadad Bomanji Irani*,[15] an identical case, where a Parsi lady after embracing Islam sought a dissolution of her marriage, observed that in the absence of any rule or authority for dealing with the case, the court was required to apply the rule of justice, equity, and good conscience on the strength of the Privy Council's ruling in *Waghela Rajsanji v. Sheikh Mosluddin*.[16]

The Court, speaking through Mr Justice Chagla, made an observation that the spouses could have happily lived together in spite of the wife's conversion to Islam, and that a dissolution of the marriage was uncalled for. With due respect to the learned judge, the Parsi Marriage and Divorce Act, 1936, as amended, does not authorize either of the spouses to become a convert to any religion, until and unless their marriage is duly dissolved by the Parsi Matrimonial Court as contemplated under the Act. Therefore, the question of the wife's seeking dissolution of her marriage as per Mahomedan law, as also the learned judge's remark that the spouses could have happily lived together despite the conversion, is ill-conceived. The wife's petition seeking dissolution of her marriage ought, therefore, to have been dismissed on the ground that she continued to be a Parsi, and seeking dissolution of her marriage on the basis of her so-called conversion does not

[15] (1948) ILR Bombay 1946.
[16] (1887) (14) 1A89.

hold water. But in a similar situation where the wife, a Hindu, who embraced Islam and sought a dissolution of her marriage, when at that time the Hindu law before its reform of the 'fiftees forbade dissolution, in *Ayesha Bibi v. Subhod Chandra*[17] and in *Rakeya Bibi v. Anil Kumar Mukherji*[18] the court, speaking through Ormond, J. in the first case and through a different Bench in the latter, by-passed the Hindu law of the defendant which forbade divorce and, instead, applied the doctrine of justice, equity, and good conscience in dismissing the petitions. If, with reference to the above two judgments, the reviewer is constrained to enter a note of sarcasm, namely, comment is surely superfluous!, he may not be committing any academic indiscretion.

Khatoon Nisa, Appellant v. State of U.P. and Others, 2002 (6) SCALE 165

The main issue in the appeals bearing on conflict of laws is whether a magistrate is invested with jurisdictional competence under Section 125 of the Code of Criminal Procedure (Cr. P.C.), 1973 (Act 2 of 1974) to grant maintenance to a divorced Muslim woman, even in the absence of a declaration as per Section 5 of the Muslim Women (Protection of Rights on Divorce) Act, 1986, by affidavit or any other declaration in writing on the part of a divorced Muslim woman and her former husband, either jointly or separately, that they opt to be governed by the provisions of Sections 125 and 128 of the Code of Criminal Procedure, 1973 (Act 2 of 1974).

[17] (1948) ILR 2 Cal 405; 49 CWN 439.
[18] ILR (1948) 2 Cal 119.

The other issues, *inter alia*, that arose for adjudication by a single judge of the Lucknow Bench of the Allahabad High Court were the determination of surplus land on the basis of Sections 3 (7) and 10 (2) of the U.P. Imposition of Ceiling on Land Holdings Act, 1960 and the constitutionality and validity of a divorce by a Muslim husband by uttering *talaq* thrice in one sitting. These two issues do not call for inquiry from the standpoint of conflict resolution.

The Constitution Bench of the Supreme Court consisting of Hon'ble Judges G.B. Patnaik, M.B. Shah, Daraiswamy Raju, S.N. Variava, and D.M. Dharmadhikari, while disposing of the appeals, made the following observation:

Subsequent to the enactment of the Muslim Woman (Protection of rights on Divorce) Act, 1986 (for short 'the Act'), as it was considered that the jurisdiction of the magistrate under Section 125 Cr. P.C. can be invoked only when the condition precedent mentioned in Section 5 of the Act are complied with in the case on hand, the magistrate came to a finding that there has been no divorce in the eye of law and, as such, the magistrate has jurisdiction to grant maintenance under Section 125 of the Cr. P.C. This finding of the magistrate has been upheld by the High Court. The validity of the provisions was before the Constitution Bench in the case of *Danial Latifi and Anr. v. Union of India* 2001, 7 Sec 740, 746; 2001 Cri LJ 4660. In the said case, by reading down the Act, the validity of the Act has been upheld and it has been observed that under the Act itself when the parties agree, the provisions of Section 125 Cr. P.C. could be invoked as contained in Section 5 of the Act and even otherwise the magistrate under the Act has the power to grant maintenance in favour of a divorced woman, and the parameters and considerations are the same as those in Section 125 Cr. P.C. It is undoubtedly true that in the case on hand, Section 5 of the Act has not been invoked. Necessarily, therefore, the magistrate has exercised his jurisdiction under Section 125 Cr. P.C. But, since the magistrate retains the power of granting maintenance in view of the Constitution Bench decision in the Danial Latifi (Supra) under the Act and since the parameters for exercise of that power are the same as those contained in Section 125 Cr. P.C., we see no ground to interfere with the orders of the magistrate granting maintenance in favour of a divorced Muslim woman.... (para 10)

'In view of our aforesaid conclusion, it is not necessary for us to examine the correctness of the finding on the status of the parties, inasmuch as the finding was merely for the purpose of exercising jurisdiction under Section 125 Cr. P.C. and has no bearing at all in deciding the status of the parties' (para 11).

'These appeals stand disposed of accordingly' (para 12).

It is of interest to note that in a recent case, namely, *Shamim Bano, Appellant v. Asraf Khan, Respondent*[19] decided by a Division Bench of the Supreme Court, the Court observed that a cumulative reading of the relevant portions of judgments of the Court in *Danial Latifi and Iqbal Bano v. State of U.P. and Another*,[20] would make it 'crystal clear' that even a divorced Muslim woman would be entitled to claim maintenance from her divorced husband, as long as she does not remarry.

Shamim Bano, Appellant v. Asraf Khan, Respondent, AIR 2010 SC 305

The facts of the case are briefly as follows:

The appellant Shamim Bano married the respondent Asraf Khan on 17 November 1993 in accordance with Muslim Shariyat Law. As the appellant was subjected to cruelty and torture by the respondent husband and his family members regarding dowry demand, she was constrained to lodge a complaint with the Mahila Thana (Ladies' Police Station) at Durg on 6 September 1994 that led to a criminal case under Section 498-A as read with

[19] AIR 2010 SC 305.
[20] (2007) 6 SCC 785.

Section 34 of the Indian Penal Code that was tried by the learned magistrate at Rajnandgaon who acquitted the accused persons of the said charges.

During the pendency of the criminal case under Sections 498-A and 34 of the Indian Penal Code before the trial court, the appellant Shamim Bano filed an application under Section 125 of the Court of Judicial Magistrate First Class, Durg, for maintenance on the ground of desertion and cruelty. While so, divorce between the appellant and the respondent took place on 5 May 1997. That led to the appellant filing a criminal case bearing No. 56 of 1997 under Section 3 of the Muslim Women (Protection of Rights on Divorce) Act, 1986 (for brevity, 'the Act') before the learned judicial magistrate First Class, Durg. The learned magistrate dismissed the case on 14 July 1999 on the ground that the appellant failed to prove her allegations of desertion and cruelty and, indeed, had been living separately out of her own sweet will and, therefore, forfeited her claim for maintenance. However, the learned magistrate, while dealing with her application preferred under Section 3 of the Act, allowed the application directing the husband and others to pay a sum of Rs 11,786 towards mahr, return of goods and ornaments besides a sum of Rs 1,750 towards maintenance during the iddat period.

Aggrieved by the order denying to her maintenance, the appellant filed a Criminal Revision petition bearing No. 275 of 1999. To her misfortune the revisional court concurred with the view expressed by the learned magistrate and upheld the order of dismissal. The appellant, therefore, had no other alternative but to invoke the jurisdiction of the High Court under Section 482 of the Code in Misc. Crl. No. 188 of 2005. A preliminary objection was raised on behalf of the respondent husband that the appellant's petition under Section 125 of the Code was not maintainable as she was divorced without her complying with the provisions contained in Section 5 of the Act. It was further contended that her initial action under Section 125 of the Criminal Procedure Code was tenable, but that the same, however, had to be overturned since she had filed an application under Section 3 of the Act for return of gifts and properties, for payment of mahr as also for grant of maintenance during the iddat period. It was also urged that the wife was entitled to maintenance during the iddat period, and as the same having been granted in the application which was filed after the divorce, grant of any maintenance did not arise in the exercise of power under Section 125 of the Code. That apart, both the parties had also advanced certain contentions aimed at obtaining factual score.

The High Court, after adverting to certain authorities, held that a Muslim woman is entitled to claim maintenance under Section 125 of the Code even beyond the period of iddat in case she was unable to maintain herself; and that where an application under Section 3 of the Act had already been moved, her right or claim to maintenance is contingent upon the exercise by her and her former husband of the option to declare by affidavit or any other declaration in writing in such form as may be prescribed, either jointly or separately, that they would prefer to be governed by the provisions of Sections 125 to 128 of the Code of Criminal Procedure, 1973 (2 of 1974); and file such affidavit or declaration in the Court hearing the application, the magistrate shall dispose of such application accordingly.

The High Court, understandably, held that the claim of the appellant wife under Section 125 of the Code would be maintainable till the time of her divorce. However, her claim to maintenance on an application filed by her under Section 3 of the Act, which had already been dealt with by the learned magistrate and allowed and affirmed by the

High Court under Section 482 of the Code, would hold 71 good for period leading up to her divorce.

LAW OF PERSONS

The High Court further held that the courts below had rightly came to the conclusion that the wife was not entitled to maintenance as she had not been able to make out a case for the grant of maintenance under Section 125 of the Code and that, therefore, the said orders deserve to be affirmed as interim maintenance that was granted during the pendency of the proceeding up to the date of divorce. The High Court, therefore, found justification for declining to interfere with the orders of the courts below in the exercise of its inherent jurisdiction.

The Supreme Court, based on the foregoing, set out two seminal issues that call for resolution. They are as follows:

(1) Whether the appellant's application for grant of maintenance under Section 125 of the Code is to be restricted to the date of divorce and, an ancillary to it, whether the filing by the appellant of as application under Section 3 of the Act after the divorce for the grant of mahr and return of gifts would disentitle her to sustain the application under Section 125 of the Code; and

(2) Whether, based on the factual situation in the present case, the consent under Section 5 of the Act, as the High Court observed, WAS imperative to maintain the application.

Mr Justice Dipak Misra referred to the previous landmark decision of the Supreme Court to strengthen his decision in the case under review, namely, *Shamim Bano v. Asraft Khan*. The first landmark decision of the Supreme Court is *Mohd. Ahmed Khan v. Shah Bano Begum*.[21] The Court,

---

[21] AIR 1985 SC 945.

speaking through Mr Justice Chandrachud, ruled that a magistrate can grant maintenance or, as the case may be, enhancement of maintenance under Section 125 of the Code of Criminal Procedure, 1973 even beyond the iddat period. Closely following on the heels of the Shah Bano decision is the decision in *Danial Latifi and Another v. Union of India*[22] which is, as it were, to overcome the legislative challenge offered by the passing of the Muslim Women (Protection of Rights on Divorce) Act, 1986, by the Union Parliament which was sequel to the Shah Bano ruling. While upholding the constitutional validity of the Act which was challenged by a writ petition filed by Danial Latifi, the former husband of the divorced Muslim woman, as violative of Articles 14, 15, and 21 of the Constitution, the Court speaking through Mr Justice Rajendra Babu held that a Muslim husband as per Section 3 (1) (a) of the Act is obligated to make 'a reasonable and a fair provision for the future of the divorced wife'. The Supreme Court further observed that the statutory obligation under Section 3 (1) (a) is inclusive in its scope and effect in that it obligates the Muslim husband to not only discharge his maintenance obligation to his divorced wife during the iddat period, but also to make 'a reasonable and fair provision and maintenance for the future of the divorced wife to be made and paid to her within the period of iddat' (per Rajendra Babu, J. as he then was). Moreover, as the said Section 3 of the Act commences with a *non obstante* clause, the judicial interpretation in the case overrides all other pre-existing laws or decisions of courts.[23]

---

[22] (2001) 7 SCC 740.

[23] See V.C. Govindaraj, *The Conflict of Laws in India—Inter-Territorial and Inter-Personal Conflict* (Oxford University Press), p. 132.

Further, Mr Justice Dipak Misra referred to the case
Khatoon Nisa v. State of U.P. and Others[24] of a Constitution
Bench of the Supreme Court of India in which it was held
that inasmuch as the parameters and considerations are the
same under Section 5 of the Muslim Women (Protection of
Rights on Divorce) Act, 1986, as under Section 125 of the
Criminal Procedure Code, even if the Muslim husband and
his divorced wife fail to invoke the option under Section 5
of the Act, a magistrate can still exercise his powers to
grant maintenance to the Muslim wife on the strength of
the ruling in Danial Latifi's case. Further, a Division Bench
of the Supreme Court in the case *Shabana Bano v. Imran
Khan*[25] observed that cumulative reading of the relevant
portions of judgments of the Supreme Court in *Danial
Latifi and Iqbal Bano v. State of U.P. and Another*[26] would
make it 'crystal clear' that even a divorced Muslim woman
would be entitled to claim maintenance from her divorced
husband, as long as she does not remarry.[27]

Thus, after highlighting the path-breaking decisions
of the Supreme Court, such as the one in Shah Bano
Begum's case where the Court ruled, as has already been
stated, that a magistrate can grant maintenance or, as the
case may be, enhancement of maintenance under Section
125 of the Criminal Procedure Code, 1973 even beyond
the iddat period; and in Danial Latifi's case, which the
reviewer chose to describe as a trendsetter, the statutory
obligation under Section 3 (1) (a) of the Muslim Women
(Protection of Rights on Divorce) Act, 1986, according to
the Supreme Court, is inclusive in its scope and effect in

---

[24] 2002 (6) Scale 165.
[25] 2002 (6) Scale 165, addendum ii.
[26] (2007) 6 SCC 785.
[27] AIR 2010 SC 305.

that it obligates the Muslim husband not only to discharge his maintenance obligation to his wife during the iddat period, but also to make a 'reasonable and fair provision and maintenance for the future of the divorced wife to be made and paid to her within the iddat period'.

It is but appropriate here to quote Mr Justice Dipak Misra to bring home the predicament of a wife when her marriage terminates. He writes thus:

Another aspect which has to be kept uppermost in mind is that when the marriage breaks up, a woman suffers from emotional fractures, fragmentation of sentiments, loss of economic and social security and, in certain cases, inadequate requisites for survival. A marriage is fundamentally a unique bond between two parties. When it perishes like a mushroom the dignity of the female fame gets corroded. It is law's duty to recompense, and the primary obligation is that of the husband. Needless to emphasise, the entitlement and the necessitous provisions have to be made in accordance with the parameters of law (Para 16 of the judgment).

Mr Justice Dipak Misra further observed, bearing in mind Khatoon Nisa's ruling, that 'seeking of option would make no difference. Therefore, the High Court erred in opining that when the appellant wife filed the application under Section 3 of the Act, she exercised her option, as the magistrate still retains the power of granting maintenance under Section 125 of the Code to a divorced Muslim woman'. Inasmuch as the proceeding was continuing without any objection and as the ultimate result would be the same, there was no justification for the High Court to hold that the proceeding after the divorce was not maintainable. It is patent that the High Court in affirming the findings of the lower courts was basically guided by the issue of maintainability.

Mr Justice Dipak Misra made it clear that he did not choose to remand the matter to the High Court for reconsideration from all spectrums as is usually the course to adopt, but that in his view it would be more appropriate that the matter be heard and dealt with by the magistrate which would afford the parties the opportunity of leading further evidence, if need be.

Dr Abdul Rahim Undre, Appellant v. Smt. Padma Abdul Rahim, Respondent, AIR 1982, Bombay 321

The facts of the case, briefly stated, are as follows:

The appellant-plaintiff, Dr Abdur Rahim Undre, married Smt. Padma, the respondent-defendant, in the United Kingdom on 6 May 1966. At the time of the marriage the plaintiff, Dr Abdur Rahim, was a Mahomedan and the defendant Padma was a Hindu. Both of them were Indian citizens, domiciled in India. Their marriage took place at the office of the Registrar of Marriages at Weymouth, as aforesaid, on the 6 May 1966 after their having given notice of intention to marry. The marriage was duly registered, and a certificate authenticating the marriage was issued, a certified copy of which was also on record. The certified copy makes known that the marriage took place under the British Marriage Act, 1949, a civil form of marriage. Four children were born of the marriage between the years 1967 and 1973. The appellant-plaintiff, Dr Abdur Rahim, in his plaint alleged that on 29 December 1969, conversion of the defendant-respondent Padma from Hinduism to Islam took place in the presence of two Mahomedan witnesses followed by a performance of Nikah ceremony. It was further alleged by the appellant-plaintiff that their relationship got strained after the birth of their fourth child, a son by name Sabir, on 21 November 1973. He further alleged that he gave talaq to the defendant in her absence from their apartment, an oral intimation of which was duly communicated to her in Paradise apartment, their residence, the same night.

The issue relating to the proprietary rights of the parties, namely, that the flat in Paradise Apartments, Bombay, that they occupied belonged to both of them, in that they acquired the said flat with the income that they earned from their respective professions. This issue of common ownership of the flat that they occupied, for which a separate suit was pending, does not touch and concern rules of conflict of laws. Accordingly, the main issue that attracts rules of conflict of laws is the issue whether the civil marriage that they contracted on 6 May 1966, before the Registrar of Marriages at Weymouth in England would lend itself to termination by a unilateral denunciation of it by the plaintiff husband, a Muslim, by pronouncing talaq against his Hindu wife Padma, the respondent in the Letters Patent Appeal of 1981.

The plaintiff-appellant, Dr Abdur Rahim, unequivocally admitted that the marriage between him and his Hindu wife, dated 6 May, 1966, was performed in England according to the British Marriage Act, 1949. That it was a civil form of marriage of monogamous character is also clear from the entry of the marriage made pursuant to the provisions of the Marriage Act, 1949. However, the presence of two Muslims who were witnesses to the marriage can by no stretch of imagination be deemed as *Nikah fasid*, that is, an irregular marriage, according to Mahomedan law in view of the fact that at the time of solemnization of the marriage the defendant was admittedly a Hindu by religion. The contention of the counsel for the appellant that the

Nikah fasid was rejected by the Court. The Court speaking
through Mr Justice Dharmadhikari observed:

It is not possible for us to accept the contention. No civil marriage
validly performed and solemnized, according to any law in force,
can be treated as a religious marriage, by introducing elements
of formalities of personal law. The presence of two witnesses of
Mohammedan faith cannot *ipso facto* convert any civil marriage
into any other form of marriage, much less a 'Nikah fasid'. As held
by the Privy Council in *AIR 1930 P.C. 31, Engene Berthiaume v.
Dame Anne Marie Yvonne Dastous*:
  'If a marriage is good by the law of the country where it
is effected it is good all over the world no matter whether the
proceedings or the ceremony which constituted the marriage
according to the law of (the) place would not constitute marriage
in the country of domicile of one or the other spouses'.

Based on the above dictum of the Privy Council,
the Bombay High Court, speaking through Mr Justice
Dharmadhikari, observed, 'The character of marriage
remains unaffected by such external factors. Because, a
civil marriage validly performed has an overriding effect
on all other religious forms of marriage'.

The Court, speaking through Mr Justice Dharmadhikari,
negatived the contention of the counsel for the appellant
that the Foreign Marriage Act, 1969, cannot have
retrospective operation to apply to a marriage, as the
present one, performed in 1966. The wording of Section
18 (1) of the Act, namely 'solemnized', according to the
learned judge, is indicative of its nature and character,
namely, that it applies even to marriages solemnized prior
to coming into force of the Act. Accordingly, sub-section
(4) of Section 18 is to be construed as grant of relief by a
court of law, and certainly not a voluntary and unilateral

act of a husband of pronouncing talaq to his wife which does not require any intervention of a court of law.

The Special Marriage Act, 1954, is secular, and marriages performed under it are monogamous in the sense that they are union for life that can only be terminated not by act of parties but by operation of law through the instrumentality of courts. In this connection, it is but appropriate to reproduce the observation of the Court. Para 23 of the judgment runs thus:

It can safely be said that (the) Special Marriage Act is in reality an Indian Marriage Act, which applies to all Indian communities irrespective of caste, creed or religion. The concept of marriage under the said Act is monogamous, that is union for life, dissoluble by judicial authorities. Under the said law all modern matrimonial reliefs are made available to both spouses in the event of breakdown of marriage on an application made to the court of competent jurisdiction. Even religious marriages can be registered under the said Act.

The Court further observed as under: (See para 23)

It cannot also be forgotten that the establishment of a secular society is the aim and goal of the Indian Constitution. Therefore, in the area and field which is secular or non-religious laws will have to be common for all citizens of India, and that is what has been done, though to a limited extent by enacting the Special Marriage Act.

English courts have shown a liberal attitude of recognizing polygamous marriages (see *Baindail v. Baindail, 1946 1 ALL ER 342, C.A.* Indian courts, too, to their credit recognize polygamous marriages when giving relief (see *Khambata v. Khambata, AIR 1935 Bombay 5*). *A contrario*, an Indian court will not recognize a polygamous marriage contracted by Christians domiciled in India (see *William Hudson v. K.M. Webster, AIR 1937, Madras 565 at 567*). Such non-recognition is based on the Indian Christian Marriage Act, 1872, as read with the Indian Divorce Act, 1969.

Smt. Mira Devi and others, Appellants v. Smt. Aman Kumari, Respondent, AIR 1962, Madhya Pradesh 212

Before going into the facts of this case, the law laid down by the High Court of Madhya Pradesh in the First Appeal No. 39 of 1958, D/31-8-1961, from the decree of the Addl. Dist. J., Ambikapur, D/-10-12-1957, the reviewer is prompted to remark that the judgment and the ratio employed by Mr Justice Shrivastava is, to say the least, novel, interesting, and intriguing.

The facts of the case are as follows:

The suit which gave rise to the First Appeal (No. 39 of 1958) was filed by the respondent Smt. Aman Kumari for possession of home farm lands lying in several villages as also for possession of movables. The respondent had also filed an appeal (First Appeal No. 120 of 1958) against the judgment in that case. This judgment was directed to dispose of both the appeals.

In the former State of Korea (now called 'Koriya') merged with the latter in the year 1948, 'Patna Zemindari' which was held by one Jagdish Prasad Singh till his death in 1942. The respondent was the widow of the deceased Jagdish Prasad Singh. He gave birth to a son Gopal Saran Singh, who, too, died in 1948. The appellant was the widow of Gopal Saran Singh, and their marriage took place on 4 July 1941 under the Special Marriage Act, 1972 (Act III of 1872) which, for brevity sake, be designated the Act of 1872. They gave birth to two sons, Vijay Prasad Singh and Lalit Prasad Singh, who figure in the appeal as appellants along with their mother Mira Davi. After the death of Jagdish Prasad Singh, the Zamindari was resumed by the Korea Darbar in 1945. However, the home-farm lands in several villages were allowed to be retained by the heirs of the zamindar. The dispute in the appeal under consideration related to those home-farm lands, the agricultural houses and other property in those villages.

The plaintiff Smt. Aman Kumari pleaded that, after the death of her husband Jagdish Prasad Singh in the year 1942, she and her son Gopal Saran Singh became the joint owners of the property; and, that after the death of her son Gopal Saran Singh in the year 1948, she became the sole owner of the property. She also pleaded that she was ousted from the property in the year 1949 by the defendants Smt. Mira Devi and her two sons. She questioned the validity of the marriage on the ground that Gopal Saran Singh was a minor when the alleged marriage between him and Smt. Mira Devi took place, and his failure to take the consent of his father Jagdish Pratap Singh rendered the marriage null and void. The second ground on which the marriage was challenged by the respondent Aman Kumari was that Gopal Saran Singh was not a Hindu but a Gond belonging to the aboriginal tribe, which rendered the alleged marriage between him and Mira Devi, a Hindu Brahmin, solemnized under the Special Marriage Act 1872, as amended in 1928, null and void.

The crucial question that needs to be answered in respect of Section 2 of the Act of 1872 is that whether non-fulfilment of the conditions laid down therein would render the marriage void *ab initio*, or whether it is valid until set aside by a court of law under Section 17 of the Act. Mr Justice Shrivastava relied upon the decision of a Special Bench of three judges of the Nagpur High Court in

Ganesh Prasad v. Damayanti, AIR 1946, 60, to reply to this query. It was held therein that Section 2 'does not lay down the conditions for the validity of the marriage, but merely prescribes the forms which have to be filled by the parties'. The employment of the word 'may' in Section 17 of the Act amply makes it clear that the court has the discretion to declare the marriage null or to dissolve it. If it does not choose to do so, the marriage impliedly is valid. Unlike Section 17 of the Special Marriage Act, 1872, Section 24 of the Special Marriage Act, 1954, categorically lays down that a marriage solemnized under the Act shall be null and void and may be so declared by a decree......' Thus, the Act of 1954, unlike the Act of 1872, does not confer upon the court any discretion to choose to declare a marriage void, or allow it to be deemed valid in the absence of such an exercise of discretion.

Strange as it may seem, as per the decision of the Nagpur High Court in Ganesh Prasad's case, all that is required is that the declarant Gur Saran Singh should profess formally before the Registrar of Marriages that he had embraced Hindu faith, and that would suffice to validate the marriage between him and his Hindu Brahmin wife, Smt. Mira Devi. This view is endorsed by the Calcutta High Court as we gather from its observation in *Dr Niranjan Das v. Mrs Ena Mohan, AIR 1948, Calcutta 146*.

Mr Justice Shrivastava quotes R.H. Gravesons's formulation of the law that governs formal validity and essential validity of a marriage in Conflict of Laws. It is, 'The essentials of a marriage are governed by the law of domicile of each party at the time of marriage....... While the formalities are governed exclusively by the law of the place of celebration applicable to the particular type of marriage celebrated' (see R.H. Groveson [1955, Third Edition], p. 131).

It is a well-known rule of Conflict of Laws that the essentials of a marriage are governed by the law of domicile of the party concerned. If that be so, the declaration that Guru Saran Singh made in the presence of the Registrar of Marriage of Wardha, where the Special Marriage Act was in force, that he professed Hinduism was considered adequate to validate the marriage he entered into with Smt. Mira Devi.

It is a well-known rule of Conflict of Laws that if a marriage is valid according to the *lex loci celebrationis* (that is, the law of the place where the marriage is celebrated), it is good the world over. Mr Justice Shrivastava draws our attention to yet another rule of Conflict of Laws that the law that governs immovable property is *lex situs* (that is, the law of the place where the property is situated). He concedes that the law that governs status is lex *domicilii*, that is, the customary rules of the Gonds prevalent in the erstwhile Korea State, that would govern the concerned parties wherever they go. All the same, he holds that 'in administering such law', the relationship would have to be taken as valid according to the law of the place of the celebration of marriage' (that is, Wardha where the Special Marriage Act was in force).

It is a well-known principle of Hindu Law that a coparcener of a joint Hindu family has an equal right as other coparceners in the enjoyment of the property that belongs to the family with a right of survivorship. But, once the coparcener gets married, it automatically brings about a severance from the joint family, even as such severance takes place on a coparcener seeking partition from the joint family. His heirs then become eligible to inherit his property on his death.

The intriguing part of the judgment lies in the conclusion that the Court arrived at, by holding that mere declaration on the part of Guru Saran Singh before the marriage officer that he was a Hindu would validate the marriage, suggesting thereby that this requirement may also be treated as procedural, the tribal customary rules as *lex domicilii*, to the contrary, notwithstanding. What emerges from the ruling is that this requirement is of a twin character referable to either of the two, the *lex domicilii* and the *lex loci celebrationis*, and that 'the marriage should be upheld if either of them supports it'.[28]

Parwathawwa v. Channawwa, AIR 1966, Mysore 100

This is a second appeal presented before the Mysore High Court for adjudication from the judgment and decree of the District Court. This appeal in respect of the property of one Siddalingiah between Parwathawwa, his first wife Siddavva's daughter, and Channawwa, his second wife. Siddalingiah died in the year 1951 and Siddavva died in the year 1956. The second marriage between Siddalingiah and Channawwa took place in the State Bombay. At that time, when the marriage took place in the State of Bombay, there was a law, entitled the Bombay Prevention of Hindu Bigamous Marriages Act, 1946, that forbade bigamous marriages among Hindus.

The respondent Channawwa was a permanent resident and a domiciliary of the State of Bombay where the marriage took place, and Siddalingiah was a permanent resident and domiciliary of the State of Hyderabad which was at that time, an independent State. She, after her marriage, joined her husband in Hyderabad and lived there

[28] See Govindaraj, *The Conflict of Laws in India*, pp. 108–9.

till his death in the year 1951. The disputed property was originally situated in the State of Hyderabad which, after the reorganization of States, became part of the State of Mysore. Hence the suit was instituted before a Munsiff's court there which dismissed it based on the Bombay Prevention of Hindu Bigamous Marriages Act, 1946. The District Court, on appeal, held the marriage valid based on the doctrine of intended matrimonial home, and decreed the respondent Chemmawwa's appeal. The present second appeal to the Mysore High Court was filed by the first wife's daughter, Parwathawwa, laying claims to the property of her father the late Siddalingiah.

Mr Justice Somnath Iyer dismissed the appeal filed by Ms Parwathawwa, thereby upholding the judgment and decree of the District Court. He virtually wrote a dissertation on the validity or otherwise of a marriage based on the doctrine of *lex loci celebrationis*, quoting leading English decisions on the subject, such as the decision of the House of Lords in *Brook v. Brook (1861) 9 HLC 193* and *Simonin v. Mallac (1860) 2 SW* and TR 67; 164 ER. 917. The learned judge further quoted the writings of jurists like Dicey and Cheshire on the subject to lend respectability to his judgment.

He, then, dwelt with at length on the subject of the dual domicile doctrine that rests on the principle that a marriage is a contractual relationship in determining its validity. In that connection, he quoted leading English cases bearing on it such as *Mette v. Mette (1859) I SW & TR 6; 164 ER 792* and *Scottomayor v. De Barros (1877) P.D.I.*

The Court of first instance of the State of Mysore, namely, the District Munsiff's Court, as pointed out earlier, allowed the suit of the plaintiff–appellant, Ms Parwatawwa, based on the Bombay Prevention of Hindu Bigamous Marriages Act, 1946, the *lex loci celebrationis*.

The learned Mr Justice Somnath Iyer, then considered the relative merits of the dual domicile doctrine and the doctrine of the intended matrimonial home. He opted for the latter in disposing of this case, thereby upholding the decision of the learned District Judge. In coming to this conclusion, he placed reliance on the weighty opinion of Bucknill, L.J. in the leading case of *De Reneville v. De Reneville (1948)*, p. 100, further fortified by the decision in *Casey v. Casey (1949)*, p. 420.

Mr Justice Somnath Iyer, while upholding the validity of the marriage based on the intended matrimonial home doctrine, made the following observation:

What emerges from the discussion is that on the question as to what law should govern capacity for marriage, there are at least three streams of thought. One view is that it is the law of celebration which overlooks the distinction between formality and capacity. The second is that it is the law of domicile of each party before the marriage which is demonstrated by the later pronouncements to be a conservative and orthodox view. The third is that the law of the intended matrimonial home is what governs capacity which has been explained as the best (para 64).

The learned judge is on the defensive in his opting for the intended matrimonial home doctrine, as one could see from his following observation. It is as set out below:

I am not unaware of the denunciation of the third view commended by Dr Cheshire. It is said that it has little practical foundation, and it is argued by the detractors that by allowing everything to hinge on intention, it opens the door to the evasion of the law. That the validity of the marriage cannot remain in suspense until the parties implemented their intention, that the assumption that the woman's domicile becomes that of the man on marriage rests on no conceivable principle and that the incapacities emanating from the law of her ante-nuptial domicile could not be disregarded is what is said against the theory (para 64).

On the strength of the ratio employed by Mr Justice Somnath Iyer thus far, it, according to him, leads to the following conclusion set out in paragraph 66. It runs thus:

The discussion made so far is about the law which governs capacity and, in my opinion, the law is the husband's domicile if not the law of the intended matrimonial home which was in the case before us, the Mitakshara School of Hindu Law in force in the erstwhile state of Hyderabad which bestowed capacity on both the spouses to marry one another. That it is so would be the end of the defendant's contention that the plaintiff was not the wife of Siddalingiah. The marriage between the plaintiff and Siddalingiah was a good and legal marriage, since the law of Siddalingiah's domicile, which was also the law of the intended matrimonial home, did not prohibit polygamy, and, so, Siddalingiah could take a second wife and the plaintiff could be that wife.

By way of a final remark on the judgment of Mr Justice Somnath Iyer, it will be apposite to say that what impressed him to validate the marriage between Siddalingiah and Channawwa was that after her marriage and she lived with her husband, taking good care of him, till his death in the year 1951.

The reviewer is constrained to remark that the whole exercise of Mr Justice Somnath Iyer in validating the second marriage of Siddalingiah based on the so-called intended matrimonial home theory, in utter disregard of the dual domicile doctrine, is nothing short of an exercise in futility. The learned judge is oblivious to the fact that the second marriage between Siddalingiah and Channawwa that took place in Bombay where there was in force the Bombay Prevention of Hindu Bigamous Marriages Act, 1946, that forbade bigamous marriages among Hindus.

The second marriage is, therefore, void *ab initio*, as it was in contravention of the anti-bigamous Act, 1946, of Bombay, the *lex loci celebrationis*, which prohibited bigamous marriages altogether among Hindus. However, he was not liable to be prosecuted for bigamy, as the pre-1955 uncodified Hindu Law permitted polygamy.

Vilayat Raj, Appellant v. Sunila, Respondent, AIR 1983, Delhi 351

The facts of this case, stated briefly, are as follows:

Smt. Sunila, the respondent, married Vilayat Raj, the appellant, on 17 June 1978. The parties were both Hindus at the time of their marriage. The marriage took place in Delhi, and the solemnization of the marriage was in accordance with the Hindu rites and ceremonies. Thereafter, the appellant Vilayat Raj became a convert to Islam and petitioned for a divorce under Section 13 (1) (ia) of the Hindu Marriage Act, 1955, on the ground of cruelty. The petition of Vilayat Raj seeking divorce from his wife Sunila was dismissed by the District Judge on the ground that the petitioner was no longer a Hindu and, therefore, could not invoke the Hindu Marriage Act seeking dissolution of his marriage. On appeal to the High Court of Delhi, Mrs Leila Seth, J. reversed the decision of the lower court, holding thereby that the appellant, despite his apostate from Hinduism by his embracing Islam was well within his right to seek a dissolution of his marriage under the said Section 13 (1) (ia) of the Hindu Marriage Act, 1955. She ratiocinated thus: 'Change of religion by one of the parties does not automatically dissolve the marriage but provides a ground to the other party for dissolution. Conversion also does not *per se* operate to deprive the party of rights which may be otherwise available to him under the Act' (Para 30 of the judgment).

The following norms emerge from the decision in this appeal. They are:

(1) A Hindu spouse of a Hindu marriage remains a Hindu for the purpose of his/her marriage despite his/her conversion to another faith;

(2) since he/she remains a Hindu despite his/her apostacy from Hinduism, his/her marriage can be dissolved only under the Hindu Marriage Act, 1955; and

(3) the above position holds good even if the conversion to another faith is by both the spouses.[29]

Promila Khosla v. Rajneesh Khosla, AIR 1979, Delhi 78

Here, in this case, the parties got married under the Hindu Marriage Act, 1955, and therefore ought to be treated as Hindu (although, it appears, the wife seemed to have professed Christianity even at that time). Subsequently, the wife declared herself a convert to Christianity, and sought a divorce under Section 2, as read with Section 19, of the Indian Divorce Act, 1869. Under the said Section 2 of the said Act, a court could grant a decree of dissolution of a marriage if the petitioner or the respondent is a Christian and the parties are domiciled in India. As both the conditions were fulfilled in this case, the Indian Divorce Act justifiably called for application. But there is a dilemma in so deciding the case for there is an alternative to it as exemplified in a subsequent ruling of the Delhi High Court in the Vilayat Raj case (discussed above), in

[29] See the Govindaraj, *Conflict of Laws in India*, p. 92.

which the Court, speaking through Mrs Leila Seth, J. categorically laid down the proposition that the spouse seeking dissolution of his/her marriage, despite any change of religion on his/her part, would still be governed by the Hindu Marriage Act, 1955, and may seek dissolution of the marriage under Section 13 (1) (a) of the Act. Mr Justice T.P.S. Chawla worked out a compromise by holding that if one of parties is a Christian and the other a Hindu, relief is available under both the laws. This compromise ruling of the Delhi High Court, it may be stated, is confined to those cases only where the parties concerned profess Hinduism and Christianity. Subscription to any other faith by either of the spouses does not attract this ruling.

Comment

A critical survey of cases bearing on the right to seek dissolution of a marriage as a result of conversion of one or other of the spouses, or both, from Hinduism to Christianity or Islam may help to unravel the attitude and approach of courts to render justice, based on law as they conceive.

In an early case, *Govardhan v. Jasodamono Dassi*,[30] where Hindu spouses of a Hindu marriage embraced Christianity and sought a dissolution of their marriage under the Indian Divorce Act, 1869, the Calcutta High Court granted the divorce, presumably based on the then Christian identity of the spouses, to the abandonment of the rules of conflict of laws. The Madras High Court in two identical cases, namely, *Peter Thapita v. Lakshmi Thapita*[31]

[30] (1891) 18 Cal 252.
[31] (1891) 14 Mad 382.

and *Perianayakam v. Pottukanni*[32] where the parties, originally Hindus, who got married under the polygamous Hindu Law (as the pre-1955 uncodified Hindu law was), sought a dissolution of their marriage after embracing Christianity. The Madras High Court, in contradistinction to the Calcutta High Court in Jasodamono's case, dismissed the petitions on the strength of the monogamous character of Christianity as reflected in the Indian Divorce Act, 1869, by recourse to rules of conflict of laws. These decisions of the Madras High Court, no doubt, have only academic interest in view of the codified Hindu Marriage Act, 1955, which under Section 13 (1) (ia) permits dissolution of a Hindu marriage which has not become monogamous.

It is of interest to note, in this connection, to draw the attention of readers to two cases of the Calcutta High Court, decided prior to the emergence of the Hindu Marriage Act, 1955, which ushered in monogamy. In the case *Aiyesha Bibi v. Subodh Chandra*[33] a Hindu wife sought a divorce from her Hindu husband after embracing Islam on the ground that under the Muslim Law she could no longer remain married to a non-Muslim. Strange as it may seem, as per the Regulating Act, 1781, ushered in by the British, the law of the defendant, namely, Hindu law, would apply which did not permit dissolution of the marriage. Ormond, J., an English judge, disallowed the dissolution of the marriage on the ground that a marriage could not be deemed a contract. He introduced the rule of justice, equity, and good conscience, based on which he dissolved the marriage. Presumably the learned judge had his apprehension that the Hindu husband may subject his wife, a convert to Islam, to cruelty and mental agony if

[32] (1894) Mad. 254.
[33] (1948) ILR Cal. 252.

the divorce did not take place. Yet in another case, *Rakeya Bibi v. Anil Kumar Mukherji*,[34] factually identical to Ayesha Bibi's case, Mr Justice Chakravarthy applied the same norms, namely, justice, equity, and good conscience, as did Grmond, J., to dissolve the marriage. In two other cases, namely, *Sayeeda Khatun v. V.M Obadiah*[35] and *Robasa Khanum v. Khodadad Bomanji Irani*,[36] decided respectively by the High Courts of Calcutta and Bombay, factually similar, in that in both the cases it was conversion of a Jewish wife or a Parsi wife to Islam and her seeking dissolution of her marriage. Lodge, J. of the Calcutta High Court and Chagla, J. of the Bombay High Court disallowed dissolution of the marriage based on the same norm of justice, equity, and good conscience of Ormond, J. in Ayesha Bibi's case as, in their opinion, the spouses could happily live together despite their Jewish wives' conversion to Islam.

After having traced cases where a divorce was sought by either of the spouses, or both, of Hindu or Jewish marriages, by their embracing Islam or Christianity, a critical appraisal of the attitude or approach of courts is called for, which a reviewer owes to the legal community.

In Vilayat Raj's case, the learned judge Mrs Leila Seth, J. while reversing the District Judge's decree of dismissal of the appellant's petition seeking divorce from his wife Sunila, held that despite the appellant's apostate from Hinduism by embracing Islam, he was well within his right to seek a dissolution of his marriage under Section 13 (1) (1a) of the Hindu Marriage Act, 1955. The learned

---

[34] (1949) ILR 2 Cal. 119.

[35] 49 CWN 745.

[36] 1948 ILR Bom. 1946.

judge employed the following reasoning in support of her holding. It runs thus:

Change of religion by one of the parties does not automatically dissolve the marriage, but provides a ground to other party for dissolution of the marriage. Conversion also does not *per se* operate to deprive the party of rights which may be otherwise available to him under the Act.

The first sentence of the above observation of the learned judge is incontrovertible, for the simple reason that it is a statement of the law bearing on the subject. On the contrary, the second sentence of the observation, read in conjunction with the holding, namely, that despite the appellant's apostate from Hinduism by his embracing Islam, he was well within his right to seek a dissolution of his marriage under Section 13 (1) (ia) of the Hindu Marriage Act, 1955. With due respect to the learned judge, the holding in this case defies law, logic, and common sense. The question may be asked as to how a person who is an apostate from Hinduism can still retain a right of seeking divorce under the Hindu marriage Act, 1955. The learned judge, it may be respectfully submitted, would have acquitted herself better had she sought for her holding inspiration from the norm of justice, equity, and good conscience.

Now turning to the case *Promila Koshla v. Rajneesh Khosla*, where the parties got married under the Hindu Marriage Act, 1955, presumably both Hindus, despite the fact that the wife, even at the time of the marriage, seem to have professed Christianity. Subsequently, the wife declared that she was a convert to Christianity, and followed it up by seeking a divorce of her marriage under Section 2, as read with Section 19, of the Indian Divorce Act, 1869. As state earlier, under the said Section 2 of the said Act, a court which is seized of the matter could grant a decree of divorce if the petitioner or the respondent is a Christian and the parties are domiciled in India. As both the conditions were fulfilled in the Khosla's case, the Indian Divorce Act, 1869, called for application. Strange as it may seem, Mr Justice T.P.S. Chawla presented a compromise solution, as stated earlier, by holding that if one of the parties is a Christian and the other a Hindu, relief could be granted by recourse to either the Christian or the Hindu law.

In conclusion, it may be stated that the above survey of cases bearing on the decisions of various High Courts on the issue of the law to be applied, where there takes place apostasy on the part of one or the other of the spouses or of both, of Hindu marriages leaves much to be desired. The reviewer feels constrained to remark that there is lack of coherence, consistency, or logic in the judicial dispensations.

Part III-2

LAW RELATING TO CHILDREN

Custody of Minors and the Role of Courts
as Parens Patriae

————

ABC, Appellant v. The State (NCT of Delhi), Respondent, AIR 2015 SC 2569 Civil Appeal No. 5003 of 2015 (Arising out of SLP (Civil)) No. 28367 of 2011

This civil appeal to the Supreme Court from the judgment of the Delhi High Court, which dismissed the First Appeal of the Appellant, an unwed Christian mother from the judgment of the Guardian Court, raises a puzzling procedural norm. It is this. Is it incumbent on the part of the unwed mother to issue notice to the putative father, while seeking from the Guardian Court a guardianship/

adoption certificate as per Section 7 of the Guardians and Wards Act, 1890? A cursory reading of Section 11 of the Act may appear to make it obligatory on the part of the unwed mother to issue notice to the putative father.

The Appellant, an unwed Christian mother, gave birth to a male child in the year 2010. She happened to be well educated, gainfully employed, and financially secure. These things enabled her to raise her minor son without any assistance from, or involvement of, the putative father. Her interest in her minor son's happiness and well-being was such that she took steps to make her son her nominee in all her savings and insurance policies. She was informed that she was under a legal obligation to declare the name of the father or get a guardianship or adoption certificate from the Guardian Court. She, thereupon, filed an application under Section 7 of the Guardians and Wards Act, 1890, before the Guardian Court seeking a declaration that she was the sole guardian of her minor son. Section 11 of the Act requires a notice to be sent to the parents of the child before a guardian is appointed. The appellant was averse to naming the father, but instead published a notice of the petition in a daily newspaper, the *Vir Arjun*, Delhi Edition. She also filed an affidavit stating that if the putative father chose to raise any objection regarding her claim to guardianship of her minor son, the same may be revoked or altered as the situation might demand. Her refusal to reveal the name and whereabouts of the putative father prompted the Guardian Court to dismiss her guardianship application on 19 April 2011. Her appeal to the High Court was also dismissed *in limini* for her failure to issue notice to the putative father of her minor son who naturally would be interested in the welfare and custody of his minor son even in the absence of a marriage between her and the respondent and, accordingly, the High

Court refused to entertain the appeal in the absence of a necessary party.

The Supreme Court, while allowing the appeal, referred to relevant Indian legislations which give primacy to the mother over the father in cases of illegitimate children. Section 6(b) of the Hindu Minority and Guardianship Act, 1956, is one such. Mahomedan law, too, accords custody of illegitimate children to the mother and her relations. Section 8 of the Indian Succession Act, 1925, which applies to Christians in India, states that the domicile of origin of an illegitimate child is that of the mother at its birth, thus according primacy to the mother over the putative father.

Mr Justice Vikramajit Sen referred to the laws of countries in the West, like the United Kingdom and the United States, which accord guardianship to the unwed mother in preference to the father. Same is the case with countries like Ireland, Philippines, New Zealand, South Africa, where primacy is accorded to the unwed mother in respect of custodial and guardianship rights in preference to the putative father.

The above analysis of civil and common law jurisdictions spanning the globe only fortifies the Indian legal system, with the exception of the law relating to Indian Christians, that primacy is accorded to the mother over the putative father in respect of guardianship of minor children born out of wedlock. In such secular matters like guardianship, it is apposite that we have recourse to Article 44 of the Directive Principles of Chapter IV of the Constitution of India, which obligates the State to endeavour to usher in for the citizens of India a uniform civil code throughout the territory of India.

On the basis of the above analysis, it will be inappropriate to impose upon an unwed mother the obligation of sending notice to the putative father, if not 'for protecting her child from social stigma and needless controversy'.

Mr Justice Vikramajit Sen recalls the classic judgment of the Supreme Court in *Lakshmi Kant Pandey v. Union of India, 1985 (Supp) SCC 701*, which was a leading case on adoption. The Court prohibited issuance of notice to the biological parents of a child aimed at preventing them from tracing the adoptive parents and the child. Although the Guardians and Wards Act, 1890, was not directly attracted in that case, yet it is important in that it reiterates the basic norm that the welfare of the child takes precedence over anyone else's, including the rights of the parents.

The learned judge in the case under review makes the judgment read colourful, by observing that, 'even in the absence of Lakshmi Kant Pandey, we are not mariners in unchartered troubled seas'. The said observation is obviously aimed at impressing upon the readers that there is yet another recent case, namely, *Githa Hariharan v. Reserve Bank of India, 1999, 2 SCC 228*, which is directly under the Guardians and Wards Act, 1890, which postulates that the interests and welfare of the child, as mentioned above, takes precedence over the rights of the parents claiming guardianship rights over the child.

If in a case, such as the present one, where the unwed mother petitions the Court claiming exclusive guardianship rights vis-à-vis the putative father, Section 11 is not attracted. In Githa Hariharan's case, the Reserve Bank of India had refused to accept an application for a fixed deposit in the name of the child signed solely by the mother. The three Judge Bench of the Supreme Court, placing reliance on Section 6 of the Hindu Minority and Guardianship Act, as read with Section 19 of the Guardians and Wards Act, 1890, highlighted the following legal norm, to quote:

....in all situations where the father is not in actual charge of the affairs of the minor either because of the indifference or because of an agreement between him and the mother of the minor (oral or written) and the minor is in the exclusive care and custody of the mother or the father for any other reason is unable to take care of the minor because of his physical and/ or mental incapacity, the mother can act as *natural guardian* of the minor and all her actions would be valid even during the life time of the father who would be deemed to be 'absent' for the purposes of Section 6 (a) of the HMG Act and Section 19(b) of the GW Act. This court has construed the word 'after' in 6 (a) of the Hindu Minority and Guardianship Act as meaning 'in the absence of ... be it temporary or otherwise or total apathy of the father towards the child or even inability of the father by reason of ailment or otherwise.' Thus this Court interpreted the legislation before it in a manner conducive to granting the mother, who was the only involved parent, guardianship rights over the child.

The right of the child to know the identity of his or her parents is 'implicit in the notion and width of (the) welfare of the child'. The said right of the child finds explicit recognition in the Convention of the Rights of Child of the United Nations, acceded to by India on 11 November 1992 which is, as it were, a vital aspect of the Universal Declaration of Human Rights, 1948.

While allowing the Appeal, the Supreme Court expressed its displeasure that the Guardian Court and the High Court had failed to discharge their primary duty as *parens patriae* to safeguard the interest and the well-being of the child born out of wedlock. Accordingly, it directed the Guardian Court to reconsider the Appellant's application without giving notice to the putative father.

Lakshmi Kant Pandey v. Union of India, 1985, SCC 701

A brief note:

This is a public interest writ petition filed by the petitioner, a senior advocate of the Supreme Court of India. It was, in fact, a letter addressed to the Supreme Court of India complaining of malpractices indulged in by social organizations and voluntary agencies engaged in the work of offering Indian children in adoption to foreign parents.

The letter of the petitioning senior advocate, as stated above, was treated by the Supreme Court as a public interest writ petition. The petitioner alleged that not only are Indian children of tender age under the guise of adoption, 'exposed to the long horrendous journey to distant foreign countries at a great risk to their lives, but in cases where they survive and where these children are not placed in the Shelter and Relief Houses, they in course of time become beggars or prostitutes for want of proper care from their alleged foster parents'. The petitioner, accordingly, sought relief restraining Indian based private agencies 'from carrying out further activity of routing children for adoption abroad' and directing the Government of India, the Indian Council of Child Welfare, and the Indian Council of Social Welfare to carry out their obligations in the matter of adoption of Indian children by foreign parents.

The Supreme Court, while disposing of the writ petition, spelt out in detail the participles and norms that ought to govern while giving Indian children in adoption to foreign parents. In the absence of legislation on the subject of inter-country adoptions, the Court laid down in detail the guidelines that ought to govern such adoptions which, by virtue of Article 141 of the Constitution of India, will have the force of law. Based upon such guidelines in the present case and in keeping with the letter and spirit of the Hague Convention on Protection of Children and Co-operation in Respect of Inter-Country Adoption, 1993, the Ministry of Social Welfare, Government of India, issued in the year 1995 revised guidelines on the subject. Needless to say, it is expected that the Union Parliament will, at the earliest, enact a comprehensive legislation on the subject of inter-country adoptions in keeping with the guidelines of the Supreme Court and the revised guidelines of the Ministry of Social Welfare of the Government of India. Of course, such a legislation by the Union Parliament on the subject of inter-country adoptions will render any recourse to the Guardians and Wards Act, 1890, on the subject otiose. Such a legislation ought to necessarily be secular and so designed as to cater to the needs of all communities of the Indian Republic.[1]

Marggarate Maria v. Dr Chacko and Others, 1969 K.L.T. 174 (F.B.)

The facts of this case, briefly stated, are as follows:

The petitioner Ms Marggarate Maria who filed a writ petition before the Kerala High Court under Article 226 of the Constitution of India for the custody of her two children wrongfully removed from her custody by the first respondent in violation of the order of a German Court, was a German national and a domiciliary of the State of Germany. Respondent number one was an

---

[1] See V.C. Govindaraj, *The Conflict of Laws in India—Inter-Territorial and Inter-Personal Conflict*, 2011 (New Delhi: Oxford University Press), pp. 130, 136, 137, and 247.

Both were Christians of the Roman Catholic faith. The
second respondent was the first respondent's father and
the third respondent the first respondent's second wife.
Both the petitioner and her husband were students of
a medical college in Germany in the late 1950s. They
got married in the year 1963, both under civil law as
also under ecclesiastical rites. Two children, a girl and a
boy, were born in the years 1964 and 1966, respectively.
Their marriage was short-lived in that both of them
moved simultaneously a German Court for divorce and
obtained a divorce from each other. A Guardianship
Court in Germany by its order vested in the mother
custody of the children and a right to visit them in favour
of the father. As there was a failure of the said order of
the Guardianship Court, a German Court decreed, by a
mutual agreement between the parties, custodial rights
to the mother and a right of access to the children to the
father. The respondent Dr Chacko removed the children
from the custody of his wife and took them away to his
native State of Kerala in India. The petitioning wife,
despite constraints, came to India and filed a *habeas
corpus* petition before the High Court of Kerala under
Article 226 of the Constitution of India, as aforesaid,
and sought restoration of custody of her children. It is
a well-known principle of conflict of laws that superior
courts, like the High Courts and the Supreme Court, are
invested with extraordinary powers as *parens patriae* to
restore the custody of the child to the spouse from whom
the child was wrongfully removed by the other spouse
that would help preserve and protect the paramount
interests of the minor.

Now coming to the merits of the case, the Kerala High
Court, in keeping with its judicial role as the preserver

and protector of the rights of the spouse who had been deprived of her custodial rights over her children by their wrongful removal by the father in violation of the order of the German Court; more so, that the said order was a faithful endorsement of the agreement reached between the warring spouses. The Court cited a catena of cases decided by courts in England, the United States, and India to establish the basic norm of Conflict of Laws that a foreign judgment, duly rendered by a court of competent jurisdiction, based on merits, is binding on a local court in keeping with the norm of comity. Section 13 (a) and (b) of the Civil Procedure Code, India, further strengthens the finality and conclusiveness of foreign judgments.

Pamela Williams, Appellant v. Patrick Cyril Martin, Respondent, AIR 1970, Madras 427

The facts of this case, stated briefly, are as follows:

This was an appeal from the order of Ismail, J. of the Madras High Court that denied the appellant Pamela William's claim that she was the natural guardian of her illegitimate female child, Mary Charmine Martin, the respondent Patrick Cyril Martin being the putative father of the child. Both belonged to the Anglo-Indian community. The respondent was the husband of the appellant's mother's sister. He seduced the appellant when she was hardly seventeen years old, taking advantage of her naivete, besides her being frail and sickly. That was in the year 1950. The illicit relationship between the appellant and the respondent continued till the year 1963. During that period she was ill-treated and occasionally beaten up by the drunkard respondent. She, then, realized her fault and joined her two maternal aunts in England. Her fourteen-year-old child continued to be in the custody of her impecunious and drunkard putative father. As stated above, the appellant by her petition presented before the Madras High Court sought guardianship of her illegitimate daughter, aged fourteen years, under Section 25 of the Guardians and Wards Act, 1890, which was dismissed by Ismail, J. on the ground that she was not the natural guardian of her illegitimate daughter. The appellant filed an appeal to a Division Bench of the Madras High Court, presided over by K. Veeraswami, C.J. and Somasundaram, J. Mr Justice Somasundaram wrote the judgment.

Mr Justice Somasundaram relied on the verdict of Lord Denning in *In re H (an infant), 1955–3 WLR 320* at p. 323, besides the statement of law relating to the guardianship of illegitimate children of Halsbury in his work, *Halsbury's Laws of England*, third edition, at p. 108 in coming to the conclusion that the mother is not only the natural but also the legal guardian of her bastard child. It is but appropriate to quote Lord Denning in the above mentioned case, as also to consider the view held by Halsbury.

Lord Denning in the said case observes as follows:

The father of an illegitimate child does not even have the status of a 'parent' to give his consent to the adoption.... The reason is that the law of England has from time immemorial looked upon a bastard as the child of nobody, that is to say, as the child of no known body except its mother. The father is too uncertain a figure for the law to take any cognizance of him, except that it will make him pay for the child's maintenance if it can find out who he is. The law recognizes no rights in him in regard to the child, whereas the mother has several rights. She has the right to the custody of it during her lifetime, until it is fourteen years of age, whereas the father has no right to its custody either during her lifetime or even after her death.

Halsbury in his above mentioned work, *Halsbury's Laws of England*, observes thus:

> The father of an illegitimate child, so long as the child remains illegitimate, is not generally recognized by the Law of England, for civil purposes. He is under no obligation to provide for the child, in the absence of any affiliation order, unless he has adopted it *de facto* or obtained an adoption order. But he may make a binding contract with the mother to contribute towards its maintenance; this is terminated by the death of the mother.

On the strength of the judicial and juristic verdict, set out above, Mr Justice Somasundaram ratiocinates thus:

> From the above, it will be seen that the tendency of modern law as stated in Eversley on Domestic Relations is to recognize the mother not only as the natural but the legal guardian of her bastard child, and entitled to its custody unless there are very reasons for displacing her rights. The mother in this case has not in any way disentitled herself either by her conduct or by neglect or by abandonment and on a long-term view of the matter. We are of the opinion that the mother should be regarded as the natural guardian of the illegitimate child, and that the change of custody from the respondent to the appellant will only be for the child's benefit.

The learned judge further observes

> 'We do not see as to why the mother is not entitled to apply for custody under Section 25 of the Guardians and Wards Act, 1890. She is not guilty of any misconduct; and all along she has been in touch with the child, sending moneys and presents....'

Further, the impecunious condition of the respondent was highlighted by his wife in her letter addressed to the appellant. That, *inter alia*, prompted Mr Justice

'As against all these, the appellant, the mother, is now well settled at London, and there is evidence to show that she has deposited substantial sums in a Bank in England even during the short stay of a few years'.

While allowing the appeal, the learned judge remarks:

Thus we are satisfied that the mother, who has not in any way disentitled herself either by neglect or by abandonment is, as the natural guardian, the fit and proper person to look after the infant. We are also satisfied that the 'tearing off the minor' from the custody of the respondent and delivering her to her mother, will not also have any psychological effect on the mind of the child. On a long-term view, the change will be for the child's benefits. We direct that the custody of the minor, Mary Charmine Martin, shall be given to the appellant, the natural guardian. The appeal is allowed and we make no order as to cost....

Mrs Jacqueline Kapoor, Petitioner v. Surinder Pal Kapoor, Respondent, Criminal Writ Petition No. 25 of 1994, D/-20-5-1994, AIR 1994, Punjab and Haryana 309

The facts of this case, briefly stated, are as follows:

Mrs Jacqueline Kapoor (the petitioner) was admittedly a German national, being born in Dusseldorf of the Federal Republic of Germany. She was the mother of a female child who was less than nine years old at the time of the petition. The respondent Mr Surinder Pal Kapoor, the petitioner's husband, was an Indian national. The petitioner and the respondent got married as per Hindu rites at Sirsa in the State of Haryana on 4 January 1984, and a female child by name Navdeep Kapoor was born of the marriage on 28 August 1985. Both the petitioner and the respondent settled down at Dusseldorf and became German domiciliaries. As ill-luck would have it, their relationship became strained, constraining Mrs Kapoor to file a petition for divorce at Dusseldorf, Germany, on 4 December 1989, and their marriage got annulled on 5 March 1993, by a Family Court at Dusseldorf. The said Family Court by its order vested the custody of the child in the mother and gave Mr Kapoor a right to visit the child every second weekend as also on holidays. The child Navdeep Kapoor was virtually assimilated to German culture and tradition in that she could only speak, write, and understand the German language. The divorce decree of the Dusseldorf Family Court which on appeal to the Higher Regional Court at Dusseldorf, Germany, preferred by the respondent, did not find favour with that court either. On his visit to the child on 1 August 1993 as permitted by the Family Court, he could manage to get from his wife the child's passport on the pretext that he would take her to the United Kingdom for a three weeks' holiday. As he failed to return to Dusseldorf even after three weeks, the wife became frantic and panicky and was compelled to lodge a police complaint at Dusseldorf. As with her approach to the police at Dusseldorf, she was left with no option but to file a writ of *habeas corpus* petition under Article 226 of the Constitution of India as read with Article 21 of the Constitution, guaranteeing personal liberty, with aid further from Sections 12 and 21 of the Guardians and Wards Act, 1890, and Sections 13 and 14 of the Indian Code of Civil Procedure.

After having engaged a Senior Advocate, Mr H.L. Sibal, who filed a written statement to the petition, the respondent took his child away from Ambala where he

had his customary residence. He failed to produce his child
before the Court despite a couple of adjournments, nor did
he contact his lawyer and, as such, the lawyer had no other
alternative but to report his no instructions to the Court.
Since the Warrant Officer appointed by the Court also failed
to trace the respondent, a non-bailable warrant of arrest was
issued by the Court. Mr Justice H.S. Bedi, the presiding judge,
directed the Deputy Inspector General of Police, Ambala
Range, Haryana as also the Commissioner of Policy, Delhi,
to ensure due investigation in the matter and production of
the respondent with his minor child before the Court on
11 March 1994. The Foreign Regional Registration officer
was also directed not to permit the respondent or the minor
Navdeep Kapoor to leave India till further orders from the
Court. As all the efforts to trace the respondent and his
minor daughter failed, the Central Bureau of Investigation,
Chandigarh was approached as the last resort to trace
them. The passports of the respondent and his child were
also ordered to be impounded and a copy of the order was
directed to be sent to the Foreign Regional Registration
Officer, Hans Bhawan, Delhi, which office was asked to
send information to the orders passed by the Court along
with their photographs to be supplied by the petitioner to
the authorities concerned of all Airports in the country. On a
request from the counsel representing the C.B.I., permission
was granted to register a case against the respondent; and
it was further ordered that the Home Secretary of the State
of Haryana and the Commissioner of Police, Delhi, would
render all help to the C.B.I. in tracing the respondent and his
child. The C.B.I., at last, succeeded in its mission of tracing
them and producing them before the Court. Thereupon, the
petitioner's counsel made a representation to the Court to
hand over the minor child to the custody of the petitioner-
mother, the child had all along been in the illegal custody of

in defiance of the various orders of the Family Court and the Higher Court of Germany.

The respondent Mr Surinder Pal Kapoor in his written statement depicted the background of his petitioning wife which he, as a dedicated Sikh husband, felt was not congenial to a healthy growth of his minor daughter. His Hindu wife's father and mother had a strained relationship which led to a divorce between them when his Hindu wife was hardly thirteen years old. Her mother further got married to another person and started living with him. That was the main reason for him to leave India and settle down at Dusseldorf with his young petitioner wife. He, for his part, started a textile business at Dusseldorf which, with the help of the Dusseldorf Government of providing him shelter and maintenance, flourished very well. His efforts at bringing up his minor child true to his Sikh tradition annoyed his wife which led to a strained relationship between them and ultimately a divorce between them. The respondent's justification for him to leave for India along with his minor daughter in defiance of the Courts' order was to wean her child away from the unhealthy influence of his divorced wife. Be that as it may.

The main legal issue bearing on conflict of laws for adjudication by the Punjab and Haryana High Court was whether the judgment of the Family Court on 5 March 1993, and of the Higher Regional Court, Dusseldorf, Germany, on 30 June 1993, are, from a legal standpoint, binding upon the respondent. The Court drew our attention to Sections 13 and 14 of the Indian Civil Procedure Code, 1908, which lay down norms for determining the binding nature of foreign judgments. As the judgments of the Courts at Dusseldorf, Germany, do not attract any of the six exceptions laid down under Section 13 of the C.P.C., they become final and binding upon the respondent.

Reference was made, in this connection, to the judgment of the Supreme Court of India in the case *Mrs Elizabeth Dinshaw v. Arvand M. Dinshaw, AIR 1987 SC 3*, where the Supreme Court observed as under:

The sudden and authorized removal of children from one country to another is far too frequent now-a-days, and as seems to me, it is the duty of all courts in all countries to do all they can to ensure that the wrongdoer does not gain an advantage by this wrong doing (see para 9 of the judgment).

Finality and conclusiveness of a judgment on the issue of custody of minor children could result only if the State within whose jurisdiction a court exercises jurisdiction adjudicates, and certainly not any other court whose exercise of jurisdiction is the outcome as it were of fortuitous circumstances. Recourse to such judicious jurisdictional norm will deter the baneful forum-shopping. This aspect was emphasized by the Supreme Court in *Smt. Surinder Kaur Sandhu v. Harbax Singh Sandhu, AIR 1984 SC 224.*

Mrs Elizabeth Dinshaw, Peitioner v. Arvand M. Dinshaw and Another, 1987, I SCC 42

The facts of this case, briefly stated, are as follows:

Mrs Elizabeth Dinshaw, the petitioner, who filed a *habeas corpus* petition before the Supreme Court of India under Article 32 of the Constitution of India for the restoration of the custody of her minor child Dustan, seven years old, from his wrongful removal by the respondent Mr Arvand M. Dinshaw who secretly brought the child from Michigan, United states to his parents' home in Pune, India. The wrongful removal of the minor child was a flagrant violation of the decree of the Court at Michigan which vested the right of custody in the mother and a grant of visitation right to the respondent on every Wednesday between 5 pm and 8 pm. Besides, the respondent was granted visitation with his minor child from Friday 6 pm until the following Monday morning every alternate weekends and then return the child to his day care centre.

Mrs Elizabeth Dinshaw was a citizen of the United States and a resident of the State of Michigan. The first respondent Mr Arvand M. Dinshaw was a citizen of India with his residence at Pune in the State of Maharashtra, where he lived with his parents prior to his migration to Michigan in 1971. He was a student of Northern Michigan University where he met the petitioner Elizabeth who was also a fellow student there. They became close friends which developed into love, and they got married on 26 February 1972, and their civil form of marriage took place before a legal magistrate at Nagaunee, Michigan. Ms Elizabeth got employed as a case-worker for the State of Michigan in Genesee County Department of Social Services, Flint Michigan. Mr Arvand Dinshaw, the first respondent, became more or less a permanent resident of the United States of America, having secured an employment as an Accountant for the Controller's Office in Genesee County, Michigan, and having obtained a permanent immigration visa. A male child, Dastan, was born to the couple on 20 August 1978 in Rochester, Michigan, United States of America, which became their marital home.

Alas! Their marriage was short-lived as differences arose between them in the year 1980, which led to the petitioner seeking a separate residence at a women's shelter in Saginaw, Michigan. She filed a petition for divorce on 2 January 1981, in the Circuit Court for the County of Saginaw, Michigan.

As the Circuit Court was convinced that the marriage between them had irretrievably broken down, a decree of divorce was granted. In the same decree the Circuit Court, as *parens patriae,* granted the petitioner custody of the child and the respondent visitation rights, as stated earlier. Then followed the respondent's taking away the child to India after having sold his house in Michigan and also resigning from his job, and the petitioner seeking restoration of the custody of the child. As the act of the respondent of the stealthily removing the child without permission from the Circuit Court amounted to contempt of court, the Court issued a non-bailable warrant of arrest of the respondent on 16 January 1986, which was later followed by a federal warrant of arrest on 28 January 1986.

The Supreme Court, speaking through Mr Justice Balakrishna Eradi, allowed the (criminal) writ petition filed by Mrs Elizabeth Dinshaw, the petitioner under Article 32 of the Constitution of India with the directions issued by an earlier order of the Court, dated 11 June 1986, for reasons set out hereunder. The learned judge relied on the decision of the Court of Appeal in England in the case Re H. (Infants),[2] where the facts were somewhat similar to this case under review, in that the wife of Scottish origin, but resident in New York, the United States for twenty years, along with her husband and her two minor sons, all three American nationals, unauthorizedly removed her two minor sons to England in the month of March 1965. Earlier, in the year 1953, she obtained a divorce from her husband from a Mexican Court which by a decree vested the custody of the children in the mother providing, at the same time, liberal access to them by their father. By a later amendment in December 1954 the Mexican Court

2 (1966) 1 All ER 886.

ordered that the minor children should reside in the State of New York under the control and jurisdiction of the State of New York. As stated earlier, the unauthorized removal of the children by their mother that took place in the month of March 1965, was a flagrant violation of the order of the Supreme Court of New York of June 1965 for their return to the State of New York. On a motion of notice given by the father in the Chancery Division of the Court in England, the trial court judge Cross, J. directed that since the children were American children, an American court was the proper court to determine the issue of custody. Therefore, it was the duty of courts in all countries to see the parent who removed his/her children out of their country did not gain any advantage by such wrong doing. Accordingly, the said foreign courts were duty bound to order that the children be returned to their native country, that is, United States, without undertaking the responsibility of going into the merits of the case to determine the issue of where and with whom the children should live. In the appeal filed against the said judgment, Willmer, L.J. of the Court of Appeal, while dismissing the appeal, quoted with approval the following passage from the judgment of Cross, J. which runs thus: 'The sudden and unauthorized removal of children from one country to another is far too frequent now-a-days, and as it seems to me, it is the duty of all courts in all countries to do all that they can to ensure that the wrongdoer does not gain an advantage by his wrongdoing'.

Cross, J. further observed:

The courts in all countries ought, as I see it, to be careful not to do anything to encourage this tendency. This substitution of self-help for due process of law in this field can only harm the interests of wards generally, and a judge should, as I see it, pay regard to the orders of the proper foreign court unless he is satisfied beyond reasonable doubt that to do so would inflict serious harm on the child.

Mr Justice Balakrishna Eradi of the Supreme Court of India expressed his wholehearted agreement with the enunciation of the principle of law of Cross, J. to be applied by courts in situations such as this. He, accordingly, disposed of the Criminal writ petition with the directions issued by the Court's orders dated 11 June 1986, for the reasons set out hereunder.

In response to the unconditional apology that the respondent tendered to the Supreme Court by an affidavit filed by him, regretting his wrongful action of removing his minor son Dastan from the lawful custody of his petitioning wife in defiance of the decree of the County Circuit Court of Michigan on 23 April 1982, conferring upon him visitation rights, the outcome of which was the termination by the said Court of his visitation rights of his wrongful action amounted to contempt of that Court, the Supreme Court advised the respondent to tender to the Circuit Court at Michigan an unconditional apology. Such a move on the part of the respondent, the Supreme Court felt, might induce the Court at Michigan to condone him and restore his visitation rights in the interest of his minor son who developed a genuine affection for his erring father. Such a course, in all likelihood, might induce the petitioning wife to extend her cooperation for the withdrawal of the warrants of arrest pending against the respondent, if a genuine approach was made by him to his petitioning wife with such a request.

This case, inter alia, exemplifies the rule of Conflict of Laws that a foreign judgment, duly rendered, is *res judicata*.

Part IV

VALIDITY OF MARRIAGE
Should It Be Deemed Omnific in Conflict Resolution of Related Issues?

———

This part of the case study deals with an interesting aspect of Conflict of Laws, namely, should validity of marriage be deemed omnific in conflicts resolution of related issues? Courts in England and India have a tendency to treat marriage and its validity as 'omnific' *vis-à-vis* related issues, such as adoption, legitimacy, rights of succession, testate or intestate, of a surviving spouse and children born of such marriage. In contrast, Courts in America have adopted an issue-based approach as highlighted in the re-statement II of Conflict of Laws of the American Law Institute which was piloted by Professor Willis L.M. Reese of the Columbia Law School. In an article, entitled 'Marriage in American Conflict of Laws' that he contributed to the *International and Comparative Law Quarterly*, London, Vol. 26 (1977), p. 952, he makes the following significant observation which runs thus:

The problem is whether the law governing the validity of a marriage should always be the same irrespective of the other issue or whether the choice of this law should depend, at least in part, upon that issue. If the latter is true, we are inevitably faced with a situation where the marriage may be good for the purpose of one issue and yet invalid for the purpose of another.

Therefore, courts in England and in India, if only they adopt an issue-based approach in respect of the issues mentioned above, the issue of the validity of marriage in resolving the dispute becomes totally irrelevant and, as such, deserves to be discarded.

Same is the case in respect of the issue of the validity of an adoption, which calls for upholding it, if it satisfies three conditions, namely the giving in adoption by the natural father, the taking in adoption by the adoptive father, and the eligibility of the adopted to be so adopted.

The first case cited in this part of the Case Study, namely, *Ratan Shah v. Bomanji, 1938 ILR, Bombay 238*, the Bombay High Court turned down the claim of the second wife of a Parsi marriage to succeed to her husband's property in Bombay, despite her marriage being in accordance with law of Baroda, *the lex loci celebrationis*, which had taken place in Baroda after a divorce that her husband sought and obtained from his first wife in accordance with the customary rule then prevalent in Baroda, known as *fargat*, simply because such a customary rule was alien to the Parsies of Bombay. Comment is surely superfluous. One wonders how the Bombay High

Court found justification for its ruling in view of the fact that all three of them, namely, the Parsi husband and his wives were domiciliaries of Baroda.

The other two cases, namely, *Kesaji v. Khaikhusroo, 1939, 41, Bombay LR 478* and *Sukdev Sahi and Others v. Kapil Dev Singh and Others, AIR 1960, Calcutta 597*, it is only a question of substitution of 'adoption' in the place of 'marriage' and the comment that was made in the first case with reference to marriage is equally the same, *mutatis mutandis*, with reference to adoption in these two cases.

The author proposes to examine the attitude and approach of courts in general, more particularly in England and India, to treat marriage and its validity as omnific vis-à-vis related issues such as adoption, legitimacy, rights of succession, testate or intestate, of a surviving spouse, and children born of such marriage.[1]

Before launching on a critical study of the hidebound attitude of courts in India of resolving disputes of related issues of a marriage and of courts in England with their characteristic insulated approach to resolving such kindred issues of a marriage, a study in comparison of courts in the United States of disassociating related issues that emerge from a marriage in resolving personal law disputes becomes compelling. It is but appropriate to take note, in this connection, the wholesome view held by Professor Willis L.M. Reese of the Columbia Law School in his path-breaking article, 'Marriage in American Conflict of Laws', *The International and Comparative Law Quarterly*, London, Vol. 26 (1977), p. 952. In that article he makes the following significant observation: 'The problem is whether

---

[1] See V.C. Govindaraj, *The Conflict of Laws in India—Inter-Territorial and Inter-Personal Conflict*, 2011 (New Delhi: Oxford University Press), Chapter 9.

in these situations (namely, of resolving related issues of a marriage treating marriage as an "all purpose concept"), the validity of the marriage should first be established independently of the other issue involved or whether the determination of the validity of the marriage should be made with reference to that issue'. Stated in choice of law terms,

The problem is whether the law governing the validity of a marriage should always be the same irrespective of the other issue or whether the choice of this law should depend, atleast in part, upon that issue. If the latter is true, we are inevitably faced with a situation where a marriage may be good for the purpose of one issue and yet invalid for the purpose of another.

With this prefatory note, the reviewer intends to critically examine the attitude of Indian courts, in particular, and English courts, in general, of resolving related issues of a marriage.

Ratan Shah v. Bomanji, 1938 ILR, Bombay 238

The facts of the case, briefly stated, are as follows:

This was a claim by the second wife of a Parsi husband to the husband's property, situated in Bombay by way of succession. Her husband, a domiciliary of Baroda, obtained a divorce from his first wife in accordance with the custom known a fargat, then prevalent among the Parsies of Baroda. The second wife of the Parsi husband claimed succession right to her husband's property situated in Bombay. The divorce that her husband obtained from his first wife by fargat was alien to the Parsies of Bombay. This factor prompted the Bombay High Court to deny to the second wife her status as the deceased husband's wife, based on which only she could claim succession rights.

Needless to say, the decision of the Bombay High Court is basically wrong for denying to the second wife her status as a legally wedded wife of her deceased husband, entitling her to claim succession right to her deceased husband's property, simply because the divorce that her late husband obtained from his first wife by fargat, as stated above, prevalent in Baroda, was alien to the Parsies of Bombay, but has not been proved to be opposed to the public policy of Bombay. In coming to such a conclusion, the Bombay High Court, needless to say, was oblivious to the divorce by fargat in accordance with the customary law of Baroda, and that the second marriage took place according to the *lex loci celebrationis*. We may here remind ourselves of the dictum of the Privy Council in England in an early adoption case, namely, that 'a clear proof of usage outweighs the written text of the law'. Moreover, the parties, all three of them, were domciliaries of Baroda. Logic and common sense would tell us that the second wife's legal status as the widow of her deceased husband and, accordingly, his heir, ought to be determined by reference to the law of Baroda and not the law of Bombay.

Keshaji v. Khaikhusroo, 1939–41, Bombay LR 478

The legal issue in this case is similar to the case discussed above, except that it is a question of the validity of an adoption in the place of a divorce and re-marriage of the earlier case. The Bombay High Court's view in this case, too, happens to be similar to the view taken by it earlier.

This was a claim for succession by an adopted son of the deceased adoptive father, a Parsi domiciled in the erstwhile State of Baroda, to his property situated in Bombay.

The adoption took place in Baroda according to the custom prevalent in Baroda among the Parsi community. The institution of adoption, no doubt, was alien to the Parsi law as practised in Bombay.

The Bombay High Court dismissed the adopted son's claim to succeed to his deceased adoptive father's property, situated in Bombay, on the ground of absence of such a law or custom of adoption in the State of Bombay.

The criticism of this decision of Bombay High Court is the same as that in the case of *Ratan Shah v. Bomanji*, namely, that an adoption that had taken place according to the law or custom of Baroda, the *lex domicilii*, cannot be set at naught by the absence of such a law or custom of adoption in the State of Bombay, the *lex fori*, unless it be that the adoption that had taken place in Baroda was opposed to the distinctive public policy of the State of Bombay. Besides, the view taken by the High Court of Bombay 'runs counter to social justice which is basic to the science of conflict of laws'.[2]

Sukdev Sahi and Others v. Kapil Dev Singh and Others, AIR 1960, Calcutta 597

This was a case of adoption by a Punjabi Brahmin gentleman, by the name Birju Maharaj, belonging to the Hoshiar District of the Punjab of a Brahmin boy, by the name Ramachandra Pandey, a permanent resident of Balia District of the erstwhile United Provinces (now re-named Uttar Pradesh), in Calcutta. The adoptive father Biru Maharaj returned to his native town in the Punjab soon after the adoption and died there in the year

[2] See Govindaraj, *The Conflict of Laws in India*, p. 151.

1941. The issue that called for determination by the Calcutta High Court was the validity of the adoption of Ramachandra Pandey by Birju Maharaj, based on which only the former could claim a right of succession to the latter's property.

Prior to the condification and secularization of the Hindu Law in the 'fiftees, the Hindu Law differed from region to region, as expounded by authoritative law givers. Whereas Punjab, like Bombay, followed the Mithakshara School of Hindu Law, the United Provinces and Bengal followed the Benares School of Hindu Law. According to the Mithakshara School of Hindu Law, followed by Punjab, a Brahmin boy could be adopted even after his *upanayana* ceremony (that is, sacred thread marriage); on the contrary, according to the Benaras School of Hindu Law, prevalent in the United Provinces and Bengal, adoption could take place only before the sacred thread marriage. If that be so, based on the religious injunction, the adoption of Ramachandra Pandey by Birju Maharaj in Calcutta stands invalidated. But, if adoption be deemed a secular affair, inasmuch as the three required conditions, namely, the giving in adoption by the natural father, the taking in adoption by the adoptive father, and the eligibility of the adopted to be so adopted, the adoption becomes valid and binding.

The outcome of the compliance with the above three conditions secures for the adopted a home which is none other than that of the adoptive father, comparable to the concept of the intended matrimonial home in the case of a marriage. The Calcutta High Court invalidated the adoption for its failure to comply with the religious injunction of the Benares School of Hindu Law that was prevalent in Calcutta. Here it becomes necessary to recall the view taken by the Privy Council in England in *Balusu*

Gurulingaswami v. Balusu Ramalakshnamma,[3] namely, that a religious injunction, such as that, one and only son cannot be given or taken in adoption, is no more than directory in nature and certainly not mandatory.

The said pronouncement of the Privy Council happens to endorse the view here taken by the author while reviewing related cases, Indian and foreign, as it (namely, the view) is founded upon two unassailable norms of social justice and the legitimate expectations of the parties concerned. The said approach in the conflicts resolution process also meets the requirement that the validity of an adoption, as in the case of the validity of a marriage, must be determined in the light of the particular issue, namely the right or claim of the adopted son to inherit the property of the adoptive father that the court was called upon to determine.[4]

---

[3] Ind. App. 113 P.C.
[4] See Govindaraj, *The Conflict of Laws in India*, p. 153.

Part V-I

FOREIGN JUDGMENTS

Recognition and Enforcement

———

The one and only case that is taken up for review in respect of foreign judgments—their recognition and enforcement, is the judgment of the Calcutta High Court in the leading case of *Chormal Balachand, Firm of Chowrahat v. Kasturi Chand Seraogi and Another*, 40 C.W.N. 592.

The legal issue that the Calcutta High Court was called up to resolve in this appeal was whether the dismissal of an action instituted by the Plaintiff-Appellant against the Defendant-Respondent for the recovery of a sum of Rs 400 as damages for breach of contract that took place in Cooch Behar State, which was a foreign State at that time outside the British Empire, in pursuance of a law in force, in that State which authorized a civil court in that State to entertain a suit if the cause of action arose wholly or partly within its jurisdiction, akin to Section 20 of the Code of Civil Procedure. The Plaintiff lost his case in both the lower civil courts in Cooch Behar on the ground that the defendants were permanent residents of the District of Gauhati in British India and, as such, aliens.

The Calcutta High Court dismissed the appeal on the ground that the jurisdictional competence of a court does not extend to a person who is neither present within its jurisdiction nor submit to the exercise of such jurisdiction by the court. For this ruling the Calcutta High Court relied upon the precedent set by the Privy Council in the leading case *Sirdar Gurdyal Singh v. Raja of Faridkote.*

Chormal Balachand, Firm of Chowrahat v. Kasturi Chand Seraogi and Another, 40 C.W.N. 592

The facts of the case, in brief, are as follows:

This appeal to the High Court of Calcutta arose out of a suit instituted to enforce a judgment pronounced by the Additional Naib Akhilkar of the Court at Danhata in Cooch Behar State. The said judgment was a foreign judgment, because Cooch Behar State was an independent State, not part of the British Indian Empire. The Additional Naib Akhilkar had the same legal status as a District Munsif of the British Indian Government. The action instituted by the plaintiff against the defendants was for the recovery of a sum of Rs 400 as damages for breach of contract. The defendants were aliens, in that they were permanent residents of the District of Gauhati in British India. The contract, however, took place in Cooch Behar. The suit was instituted before the Court of Danhata in

Cooch Behar State on the strength of a law in force in Cooch Behar State which authorized a civil court in that State to entertain a suit, other than a suit for immovable property, if the cause of action arose wholly or partly within its jurisdiction, akin to Section 20 of the Code of Civil Procedure in India.

The plaintiff had lost his case in both the courts below. Hence, he preferred an appeal to the High Court seeking recognition and enforcement of the decree of the Danhata Court. Mr Justice Mitter of the Calcutta High Court dismissed the appeal with costs. The learned judge relied on principles laid down in leading cases from England such as *Rousillon v. Rousillon, L.R. 14 Ch. Div 351 at p. 371, 1880), Schibsby v. Westenholz, 1870, L.R. 6 Q.B. 1155, Price v. Dewhurst, 1837, 8 sim. 279), Buchanon v. Rucker, 1808, 9 East 192*, and, in particular, *Sirdar Gurdyal Singh v. Raja of Faridkote, 1894, A.C.670.* The Privy Council in the last of the cases stated above held that no territorial legislature can give jurisdiction, which any foreign court ought to recognize against absent foreigners who owe no allegiance or obedience to the power which so legislates.

The judgment of the Calcutta High Court dismissing the appeal presented before it for adjudication needs no further comment, in that the jurisdictional competence of a court does not extend to a person who is neither present within its jurisdiction nor submit to such exercise of jurisdiction by the court.

The Privy Council, speaking through Lord Selborne in the case *Sirdar Gurdyal Singh v. Raja of Faridkote* ratiocinated thus: 'In a personal action ... a decree pronounced *in absentem* by a foreign court, to the jurisdiction of which the defendant has not in any way submitted himself is by International Law an absolute nullity. He is under no obligation to obey it, and it must be regarded as a mere nullity by the court of every nation....'

This ratiocination by Lord Selborne is a fitting finale to the review of the case *Chormal Balachand, Firm of Chowrahat v. Kasturi Chand Seraogi and Another.*

Part V-2

FOREIGN ARBITRAL AWARDS AND FOREIGN JUDGMENTS BASED UPON SUCH AWARDS

A Juridical Inquiry

———◆———

This part deals with the legal status of a foreign arbitral award vis-à-vis a local arbitral award. Whereas in the case of a local arbitral award there takes place an automatic merger of the original cause of action with the award, which is not the case with a foreign arbitral award, in that a suit may have to be instituted in a local court of the concerned state for its recognition and enforcement as is the case with a foreign judgment. Further, any procedural formality of the State where the award was rendered for its confirmation by a superior court does not relegate a foreign award to an inferior legal status.

An arbitral award duly rendered between the parties is *res judicata* even as a foreign judgment. Any procedural requirement for its ratification or confirmation by a superior court of the country concerned does not devaluate or diminish its finality and conclusiveness, provided the arbitral award fulfils three conditions, namely, submission of the parties to arbitration, conduct of arbitration in accordance with the submission, and, finally, its validity by the law of the forum.

Besides, the Case Study deals with cases illustrative of the principle that selection of the forum or jurisdiction of a court, contrary to the forum or jurisdiction that the parties to the commercial arbitration have opted for in their contract, like the balance of convenience or the interests of justice, are taken care of.

In the leading case *Oil and Natural Gas Commission v. Western Company of North America, 1987, AIR 674,* the Supreme Court reiterated the principle that finality is attributed to a foreign arbitral award only on its being transformed into a judgment or decree of a court as per Section 17 of the Indian Arbitration Act, 1940. This requirement for imparting finality to a foreign arbitral award has been done away with by the passing of the Arbitration and Conciliation Act, 1996. We may conclude the review of the case with following note:

The outcome of the Arbitration and Conciliation Act, 1996, is that the requirement of a judgment or a decree passed in terms of the award is a prerequisite for its enforcement has been done away with and, that, accordingly, an arbitral award becomes final and binding on the parties which could be enforced as if it is a decree of a court.

–Mr A.K. Ganguly, Sr. Advocate, Supreme Court of India.

Badat and Co., Bombay v. East India Trading Co., AIR 1964, SC 538

This was the first test case on foreign arbitral awards brought before the Supreme Court of India for adjudication. Before dealing with facts of the case and the law laid down by the Court, we need to utter a few words by way of prefatory note that would help a critical appraisal of the judgment rendered by the Court.

The difference between a local judgment or, as the case may be, a local arbitral award vis-à-vis a foreign judgment or a foreign arbitral award is that the former, namely, a local judgment or a local arbitral award, is *res judicata* in the sense that there takes place an automatic merger of the local judgment or a local arbitral award into the original cause of action. That is not the case with a foreign judgment or a foreign arbitral award. In the case of a foreign arbitral award, the procedural norm of the country where the award is rendered invariably requires a formal confirmation by a higher judiciary. Whether it is a foreign judgment or a foreign arbitral award, for its enforcement in a country other than the country where the judgment is given or the award rendered, a suit may have to be instituted in the designated court of that country for its recognition and enforcement. Viewed from a legal standpoint, a foreign judgment, validly rendered requires, based on comity, the institution of a suit in the court of the concerned country by the successful party for its recognition and enforcement. That is not the case with a foreign arbitral award, in the sense that the successful party has the option either to sue on the basis of the foreign award or on the basis of the original cause of action that resulted in the award. The said option, however, should not be mistaken to relegate a foreign arbitral award vis-à-vis a foreign judgment to an

Trading Co., as aforesaid, was the first test case that came
up before the Supreme Court for adjudication.

The facts of the case, briefly stated, are as follows:

The plaintiff respondent, the East India Trading Co.,
incorporated in the State of New York, entered into
a contract with the defendant appellant company, a
partnership firm carrying on import and export business
in Bombay, upon the terms of the American Spice Trade
Association. One of the terms of the contract entered into
between the Bombay Co. and the American East India
Trading Co. was that all questions and controversies and all
claims arising thereunder should be submitted and settled
by arbitration and that the award made by the arbitrators
should be final and binding on the parties. Disputes arose
between the parties on two contracts entered into by
them. As per the terms of the contract, the said disputes
were referred to arbitration which culminated in two
ex parte awards against the defendant-appellant which
were confirmed by a judgment of the Supreme Court of
New York to facilitate their enforcement in a foreign
court. The plaintiff-respondent, thereupon, filed a suit
against the defendant-appellant on the original side of the
Bombay High Court for the enforcement of the awards
on the basis of the judgment of the Supreme Court of
New York or, alternatively, on the basis of the awards
themselves. Having lost its case in the Bombay High
Court, the defendant Company preferred an appeal before
the Supreme Court of India which allowed the appeal. The
two grounds based on which the Supreme Court allowed
the appeal are set out below.

(1) The cause of action for the plaintiff's suit on the original
    side of the Bombay High Court, in that it rested on the

judgment of the New York Supreme Court, must be taken to have arisen outside the original jurisdiction of the Bombay High Court, and that the suit based on that judgment to the exclusion of the original cause of action must be held to be beyond the jurisdiction of the High Court of Bombay.

(2) Secondly, the arbitral awards, lacking as they do, finality or conclusiveness as per *lex fori* (that is, the law of New York) till they actually culminated in a judgment, cannot furnish a valid cause of action for the suit before the Bombay High Court.

The ratio employed by the Supreme Court both in respect of the lack of jurisdiction for the Bombay High Court to entertain the suit, as also that the arbitral award in the absence of its confirmation by the Supreme Court of New York could not furnish a valid cause of action for a suit seeking its enforcement is, with due respect to the Supreme Court of India, fallacious for the reasons set out below:

Ratio number one contradicts the doctrine of obligation enshrined in Section 13 (a) and (b) of the Indian Civil Procedure Code, 1908. If the said doctrine of obligation is understood aright, the original cause of action as per rules of conflict of laws automatically merges with the award which itself provides a cause of action for its being entertained in the suit brought before the Bombay High Court. The further confirmation of the award by the Supreme Court of New York in accordance with the procedural law of New York, imparting to it a new cause of action, if I may say so, is no more than a formality. If that be so, I may respectfully submit, the arbitral award enjoys the same legal status as the judgment of the Supreme Court of New York which is deemed to confirm the award and lend finality to it. Further, 'the technical procedural rule of nexus between jurisdiction and cause of action has no relevance whatsoever to actions brought before municipal courts for enforcement of foreign judgments[1] and, as for that, foreign arbitral awards.

Ratio number two of the Supreme Court of India, which relegates foreign arbitral awards to an inferior legal status unlike foreign judgments, is equally fallacious. The fact of the matter is that a foreign arbitral award, even as a foreign judgment, may by itself furnish a valid cause of action for a suit instituted for its enforcement. Any procedural requirement of a country for a further ratification or confirmation of the award, as in this case, by the Supreme Court of New York could neither belittle its importance nor make it any the less binding between the parties. An arbitral award duly rendered between parties is *res judicata* even as a foreign judgment. Any procedural requirement for its ratification or confirmation by a superior court of the country concerned does not devaluate or diminish its finality and conclusiveness, provided the arbitral award fulfils three conditions, namely, submission of the parties to arbitration, conduct of arbitration in accordance with the submission, and finally, its validity by the law of the forum. It is evident that all the three conditions set forth above are present in respect of the award in this case and, as such, the award itself could furnish a valid cause of action for the suit instituted in the Bombay High Court for its enforcement.[2]

The stand taken here is fortified by the decision of the Queen's Bench Division of the High Court of England,

---

[1] See V.C. Govindaraj, *The Conflict of Laws in India: Inter-Territorial and Inter-Personal Conflict*, 2011 (New Delhi: Oxford University Press), pp. 217–18.

[2] Govindaraj, *The Conflict of Laws*, 2011.

despite its repudiation by the Supreme Court of India, in the case *Union Nationale Des Cooperatives Agricoles v. Robert Catterall and Co. Ltd., 1959 2 QB 44.*

The High Court of England in the above case aptly observed that 'The fact that the award was not directly enforceable in Denmark until judgement of the Danish courts had been obtained did not prevent the award being a final award within Section 37 (1) (d) and, accordingly, Section 36 (1) applied to it and it was enforceable in the same way as an English award'.

Forum for Arbitration, Whether Irrevocable— Could the Doctrine of Balance of Convenience Outweigh the Forum Agreed upon by the Concerned Parties?

The Black Sea Steamship U.L. Lastochkina Odessa, U.S.S.R. and Another, Petitioners, v. The Union of India, Respondent, AIR 1976, AP 103.

This case assumes importance based on the principle that the forum chosen by the parties in their agreement to resolve their dispute for any violation of their contract is not so sacrosanct, if their dispute is adjudicated upon in the court of a different country to the jurisdiction of which the parties are amenable, based on the twin principles of balance of convenience, coupled with serving better the ends of justice.

This was a civil revision petition brought before a Division Bench of the High Court of Andhra Pradesh from the judgment and decree of the Subordinate Judge of Visakhapatnam, dismissing the petition filed against the respondent for the action brought before it by the respondent contrary to the forum agreed upon by the parties for resolution of any dispute that may arise between them! The facts of the case, briefly stated, are as follows:

The Union of India purchased certain quantity of ammonium sulphate in the State of U.S.S.R. and entrusted it to the firsst petitioner, the Steamship organization of Odessa in that State, for transport to Visakhapatnam, a port in the east coast of India. The second petitioner, an agent of the first petitioner, was looking after the steamship's affairs in India and figured as the second defendant.

On arrival of the consignment at Visakhapatnam, the representatives of the Union of India (Respondent) found certain bags were damaged as also there was a shortfall of ammonium sulphate. A suit was, therefore, instituted against both the petitioners before the subordinate judge of Visakhapatnam to recover the amount with interest at six per cent per annum. It was stated in the plaint that the cause of action arose at Odessa and also at Visakhapatnam. It may also be stated that the Port Trust at Visakhapatnam issued a short landing certificate to the respondent. Of the several terms and conditions incorporated in the bill of lading for the exercise of jurisdiction by a court, condition No. 26 was vital which runs thus: 'All claims and disputes arising under and in connection with the bill of lading shall be judged in the U.S.S.R'.

On the basis of the above condition, the petitioners, namely, the principal and its agent in India, filed a joint statement challenging the jurisdiction of the Court at Visakhapatnam to entertain the suit in contravention of the vital condition No. 26 of the bill of lading. The learned Subordinate Judge of Visakhapatnam rejected the objection of the petitioners which he treated as a preliminary issue. The Court distinguished all decisions relied upon by the petitioners and held that when two courts can take cognizance of a dispute and try the case, the parties were at liberty to choose anyone of the two forums for instituting a case, and that such an exercise of choice would not be in contravention of Section 28 of the Indian Contract Act. For coming to this conclusion, the Subordinate Judge relied upon two decisions of the Calcutta High Court. The Court also cited a decision each of the Andhra Pradesh High Court and the Madras High Court to spell out that such exercise of choice of forum by the parties is not repugnant to Section 28 of the Indian Contract Act. The Court also drew our attention to the decision of the Supreme Court in *Hakam Singh v. Gammon (India) Limited, AIR 1971, SC 740,* with a view to establishing the proposition that the parties are at liberty to choose to institute action in anyone of the courts spelt out in their agreement which have inherent jurisdiction to try the case. Such an exercise of choice by the concerned parties is certainly not repugnant to Section 28 of the Indian Contract Act. All the same, we have to bear in mind that such an exercise of choice of courts in all the above cases was among Indian courts.

The principle of exercise of choice cannot be different even if the courts exercising jurisdiction are in different countries. The Andhra Pradesh High Court cited several decisions of courts in England and also in the United States to strengthen its ruling. We have to bear in mind that the said principle of choosing the forum to institute action is based on the precepts of balance of convenience as also serving the ends of justice.

To fortify its dismissal of the revision petition, thereby upholding the view taken by the lower court, the High Court of Andhra Pradesh had recourse to the opinion of the eminent jurist G.C. Cheshire who, in his great treatise on Private International Law, holds the following view:

As distinct from the express or implied choice of the proper law, the express choice of a foreign tribunal is not absolutely binding. In accordance with the excellent principle that a contractual undertaking should be honoured, there is, indeed, a *prima facie* rule that an action brought in England in defiance of an agreement to submit to arbitration abroad will be stayed, the Cap Blanco (1913) p. 130, *Austrian Lloyd Steamship Co. v. Gresham Life Assurance Society Ltd., (1903) 1 KB 249)*, but, nevertheless, the court has a discretion in the matter and where the parties are amenable to the jurisdiction as, for example, where the defendant is present in England, it will allow the English action to continue if it considers that the ends of justice will be better served by a trial in this country (The Athance (1922) 11 LLL Rep. 6). The Fehmarn, (1958) 1 WLR 159).

On the strength of the above view of Cheshire, the High Court of Andhra Pradesh made the following observation:

The learned author Cheshire is thus of the opinion that once the parties are amenable to (the) jurisdiction of a Court, it is open to the Court in a particular country, though the parties have agreed to have their actions adjudicated upon in a different country to entertain the cause and adjudicate upon it, if it considers that the ends of justice will be better served by a trial in its country.

It is but appropriate to set out verbatim the ratio employed by the High Court in support of the view taken by it in paragraphs 13 and 14 of the judgment, and also the concluding remarks depicting the reason behind the preference shown to the entertainment of the dispute by the Visakhapatnam Court, and not by a Odessa Court despite the condition No. 26 of the bill of lading.

The above discussion yields the firm conclusion that it is perfectly open to the court to consider the balance of convenience, the interests of justice and like circumstances, when it decides the question of jurisdiction of a court, in the light of a clause in the agreement between the parties choosing one of the several courts or forums which were available to them. Indeed, such a consideration is essential in the interests of international trade and commerce for the better relations between the countries and peoples of the world (para 13 of the judgment).

The Court further observed:

Applying the above principle to the circumstances of the present case, it is abundantly clear that the balance of convenience and the interests of justice are in favour of adjudicating upon the respondent's dispute before the Visakhapatnam Court. The shortfall was discovered after the consignment was landed at Vishakhapatnam Port. The said Port authorities gave a certificate to the respondent in regard to the shortfall. Consequently, all the material evidence regarding the shortfall and the claim in respect thereof has to be gathered from Visakhapatnam. Needless to point out that it is positively inconvenient and highly expensive to take all this material and all the witnesses from Visakhapatnam all the way to Odessa in the U.S.S.R. Further, the sum is so small that it would be unwise for any person to spend much more than the amount claimed in the suit. Equally important is the consideration that the 1st petitioner is not in any way inconvenienced because the 2nd petitioner is its agent at Vishakhapatnam who looks after not only the actual landing of the consignment from the ships but also all its affairs at Vishakhapatnam. With the result the 1st petitioner undergoes no inconvenience at all because the 2nd petitioner can easily look after not only this legal matter but all its affairs. The facts of this case thus clearly show that the balance of convenience and the interest of justice are in favour of the Vishakahapatnam Court deciding the suit (para 14 of the judgment).

While dismissing the revision petition the High Court of Andhra Pradesh made the following significant observation:

Further, in this particular case there is another additional feature which would support the view we are taking. A joint and several decrees is sought against both the petitioners. It cannot be visualized now what the ultimate decree in the suit would be, and if there is a decree, whether it would be against both the petitioners or against one particular petitioner. If it is Odessa Court there would be no cause of action against the 2nd petitioner, since it is the 1st petitioner's agent, only in Vishakhapatnam. So, Odessa Court would have no jurisdiction to entertain a suit against the 2nd petitioner. Thus, from any perspective, we have no hesitation to hold that Vishakapatnam Court has jurisdiction to entertain the suit despite condition No. 26 of the Bill of lading (para 15 of the judgment).

Far East Steamship Line, Vladivostok, U.S.S.R. and Others ... Petitioners v. The Union of India Represented by the Regional Director (Food) Southern Region, Madras ... Respondent, C.R.P. No. 2044 of 1969. 10 May 1972. *The Madras Law Journal* Reports, 1972, 578

This case does not call for any detailed comment, as the precepts for choosing the forum or the jurisdiction of a court, contrary to the forum or jurisdiction that the parties to the commercial arbitration have opted for in their contract, like the balance of convenience or the interests of justice and the circumstances are similar.

The facts of the case are briefly as follows:

The question that arose for consideration in this civil revision petition presented before the Madras High Court for adjudication from the judgment and decree of the City Civil Court of Madras, dismissing the plea of the petitioning defendants of lack of jurisdiction for the said court for violating the foreign jurisdiction clause in their agreement, based on the so-called factors like balance of convenience, serving interests of justice, and the like.

The Division Bench of the Madras High Court, consisting of the then Chief Justice and a puisne judge, dismissed the civil revision petition of the defendants, upholding thereby the dismissal order of the City Civil Court of Madras based on the norms of balance of convenience, serving the interests of justice and similar others. If this be the attitude of courts, the defendants contended, it may lead to some of the leading shipping and air companies to choose not to do business at any of the Indian ports.

Two clauses in the bill of lading are of vital consideration in the determination of the civil revision petition. They read as follows:

26. All claims and disputes arising under and in connection with this bill of lading shall be judged in the U.S.S.R.

27. All questions and disputes not mentioned in the bill of lading shall be determined according to the Merchant Shipping Code of the U.S.S.R.

As the parties to the contract explicitly agreed in clause 27 of the bill of lading to be governed by the Merchant Shipping Code of the U.S.S.R. (that is, the *lex causae*), the Union of India could not be bailed out of its obligation to be so governed by the Code. But the forum that they have chosen under the contract in the bill of lading, namely, that their dispute ought to be brought only before a court in the U.S.S.R for determination, ought not to be deemed irrevocable in that it is subject to considerations such as balance of convenience, meeting the ends of justice under the circumstances of the case and the like. For this proposition the court relied on the law laid down in the case, *Messers Black Sea State Steamship Line v. The Minerals and Metals Trading Corporation of India Limited, 1970 I M.L.J. 548.* To fortify its stand, the Court cited English cases as illustrations.

While dismissing the civil revision petition of the petitioners, the Court made the following observation.

In the view of that Court, (viz., the English Court), therefore, the situation in the conflict of laws and jurisdictions does not demand that a foreign clause should invariably be enforced as always binding on the parties thereto. We do not think that such a view may necessarily hamper or obstruct or impede international trade. The claim in this case is under Rs 5,000/- and the expense involved in driving the Union of India to Russian Courts will far exceed the amount of the claim. That, in our opinion, is one of the circumstances which can legitimately be taken into account in enforcing a foreign jurisdiction clause. Also, we think, that by allowing the Union to sue in this country, no prejudice will be caused to the defendants. It is not suggested before us that evidence on the issues of fact to be decided will not be available for trial at Madras, and on that account, there will be any relative inconvenience. We dismiss the petition with costs.

Comment

In short, what the Court chose to lay claims to in deciding the petition is that while parties to the shipment contract are bound by the *lex causae*, the law that governs their contract, their choice of the *lex fori*, namely, the jurisdiction of the court they chose for resolving their dispute is not irrevocable, in that it may be subjected to norms such as balance of convenience, besides considerations like meeting the ends of justice, its effect on international trade, and other similar circumstances.

Oil and Natural Gas Commission v. Western Company of North America, 1987, AIR 674

The facts of the dispute between ONGC and Western Company of North America are briefly as follows.

The Plaintiff-Respondent, the Western Company of North America, entered into an agreement with the Defendant-Appellant, the ONGC, for carrying out drilling operations for the benefit of the latter. The contract provided settlement by arbitration for resolving disputes in accordance with the Indian Arbitration Act, 1940 read with relevant rules. Disputes having arisen between the parties, the Western Company of North America referred the same for resolution, London being the venue as per their agreement. The arbitration tribunal was composed of two arbitrators and an umpire. As the two arbitrators could not reach any accord between them, they referred the dispute to the umpire for its resolution. The umpire straight away gave an interim award even without hearing the disputants (non-speaking in nature), his justification for doing so being that he was present all through the hearing. Thereafter, at the request of the Respondent, the Western Company of North America, the umpire authorized one Mr Singhania to file the award in the appropriate court in India. Accordingly, Mr Singhania lodged the award in the Bombay High Court. Subsequently, the umpire rendered a supplementary award, designated the 'final' award, as to costs. That, too, was lodged in the Bombay High Court by the umpire at the instance of the Respondent. A month later, the

Respondent, the Western Company, lodged a plaint in the United States District court, *inter-alia*, seeking an order (1) confirming the two awards rendered by the umpire as also (2) a judgment against the ONGC, the Appellant, before the Supreme Court of India, for a sum of Rs 256,815.45 by way of interest until the date of the judgment and costs, and so on. Subsequently, the ONGC, the Appellant, filed a petition before the Bombay High Court under Sections 30 and 33 of the Indian Arbitration Act, 1940, for setting aside the awards for failure to follow the procedural due process and of the failure of the two arbitrators of giving a notice in writing to the umpire about their disagreement which would have facilitated assumption by the umpire of his role as such. Neither did the umpire hold any proceedings nor afford the ONGC a hearing after his assumption of his role as umpire. The Appellant, ONGC, also prayed for the grant of an interim order restraining the Western Company from proceeding further with the action instituted in the U.S. Court. The learned single judge of the Bombay High Court granted an interim restraint order *ex parte*, which he was constrained to vacate after hearing the parties. This led to the appeal to the Supreme Court of India by special leave.

The Supreme Court of India reiterated the ratio it employed in the Badat case by way of interpretation of Article V (1) (e) of the New York Convention. We may here draw the attention of the readers that India happens to be a party to the Geneva Convention of 1937 as well as the New York Convention of 1958. It needs also to be pointed out the latter of the two Conventions is an improvement vis-à-vis the former.

The said Article V (1) (e) of the New York Convention, in the opinion of the Supreme Court, gives rise to the following, namely, that the enforceability must be determined as per the law applicable to the award (emphasis added), or, in other words, the proper law;

(ii) French, German, and Indian courts have taken the view that the enforceability as per the law of the country which governs the award is essential (sic) precondition for asserting that it has become binding under Article V (1) (e) see (1987) 1 SCC 496, p. 514. The ratio of the Supreme Court, set out above, is in accord with Section 17 of the Indian Arbitration Act, 1940, which attributes finality to an award only on its being transformed into a judgment and decree of a court. This view of the Supreme Court, as pointed out by the reviewer in Badat case, is contrary to the well-established rule of Conflict of Laws which attributes finality to an arbitral award equating it with a foreign judgment duly rendered. Section 35 of the Arbitration and Conciliation Act, 1996, which superseded the Indian Arbitration Act, 1940, lays down in Section 35 that an arbitral award shall be final and binding on the parties and persons claiming under it respectively. Section 36 further unambiguously lays down that '(w)here the time for making application to set aside the arbitral award under Section 34 has expired, or such application having been made, it has been refused, the award shall be enforced under the Code of Civil Procedure, 1908 (5 of 1908) in the same manner as if it were a decree of a court'.

Appropriately, we may conclude the case under review on the following note:

The outcome of Arbitration and Conciliation Act, 1996, is that the requirement of a judgment or a decree passed in terms of the award is a prerequisite for its enforcement has been done away with and, that, accordingly, an arbitral award becomes final and binding on the parties which could be enforced as if it is a decree of a court.[3]

Bhatia International v. Bulk Trading (2002) 4 SCC 105: All provisions of Part I of the Arbitration and Conciliation Act, 1996 were to be applicable to foreign seated arbitrations, unless expressly or impliedly excluded.

BALCO v. Kaiser Aluminium (2012) 9 SCC 552: A constitution bench of the Supreme Court of India prospectively overruled the decision in *Bhatia International* and held that Part I of the Arbitration and Conciliation Act, 1996 would not be applicable to foreign seated arbitrations.

Reliance Industries v. Union of India (2015) 13 SCC 562: In this case the parties had agreed for the venue of arbitration to be London. This, combined with the choice of law being English law, was the basis for the Court to hold that Part I of the Arbitration and Conciliation Act, 1996 would not be applicable.

The 2015 amendment to the Arbitration and Conciliation Act, 1996 has changed the position of law, as Section 2(2) of the said Act now provides that the provisions pertaining to interim reliefs and recording of evidence (Sections 9, 27, and 37) contained in Part I of the Act would be applicable even to foreign seated arbitrations.

[3] See Amal K. Ganguli, *India and International Law* (Martinus Nijhoff Publishers, 2005), pp. 319, 335–6.

Note: Incorporate the three Supreme Court decisions delivered in the years 2002, 2012, 2015 respectively, as also the 1915 amendment to the Arbitration and Conciliation Act, 1996, which makes the procedural due process applicable even to foreign seated arbitrations.

Part VI

PROPERTY

This part highlights the principle that municipal courts refrain from exercising jurisdiction in respect of title to, or of any kind of right or interest in, foreign immovables. A municipal court shall not entertain an action for declaration to title to or division of foreign immovables or, as for that, possession of such immovables. The same is the case with proceedings, if the issue involved is basically one of title of any kind in relation to foreign immovable, such as a right to share in the annual allowance charged on the revenue of a foreign village, or of a right to seek partition of a foreign land.

The case chosen to highlight the principle set out above is the case *M.Y.A.A. Nachiappa Chettiar v. M.Y.A.A. Muthu Karuppan Chettiar, AIR 33, 1946 Madras 398.*

This case brings out in bold relief the well-known principle of Conflict of Laws 'that municipal courts refrain from exercising jurisdiction in respect of title to, or of any kind of right or interest in, foreign immovables. An Indian court shall not entertain any action for a declaration of title to or division of foreign immovables or, as for that, possession of such immovables'. The same is the case with proceedings, if the issue involved is basically one of title of any kind in relation to foreign immovable, such as a right to share in the annual allowance charged on the revenue of a foreign village, or of a right to seek partition of a foreign land'.[1]

The facts of the case, briefly stated, are as follows:

The plaintiff-appellant and the defendant 1-respondent were the sons of M.Y.A. Annamalai Chettiar. The plaintiff was the son of the second wife of Annamalai Chettiar and the defendant 1, the son of his first wife. Defendants 2 of 4 were the sons of defendant 1. Defendant 5 was the mother of the plaintiff and defendant 6 his sister. Annamalai died on 18 September 1926. Before his death he executed a will, dated 21 August 1926, by which he appointed two persons as executors of his money-lending firm in Puttalam in Ceylon and movable and immovable properties in Karaikudi. The further details of the testament of M.Y.A.

---

[1] See V.C. Govindaraj, *The Conflict of Laws in India— Inter-Territorial and Inter-Personal Conflict* (Oxford University Press, 2011), p. 157.

Annamalai do not call for portrayal from the standpoint of Conflict of Laws. Even the deed (that is, *muchilika*) jointly executed by the plaintiff and the defendant 1, the two sons of the executor, in the year 1940, entrusting to the panchayat (that is, the local administration) the duty of partitioning the joint family properties of the deceased executor became infructuous as it failed to take place.

The plaintiff, the son of the second wife of the deceased Annamalai, alleged that his father had no power of disposition, as the properties belonged to the joint family, and the testament was consequently void. He also averred that the provision in the testament allotting immovable properties worth about Rs 35,000 to defendant 1 as extra share was invalid and not binding on him.

Defendant 1 pleaded, *inter alia*, that the court had no jurisdiction to entertain the suit in so far as it related to immovable properties situated in Ceylon, now renamed Sri Lanka, and that the plaint made no mention of the immovable properties of considerable value in Ceylon, either acquired with the profits of the money-lending business, or forming the assets of the firm. Defendant 1 further stated that it was well within the competence of his father to dispose of his properties in Ceylon by testament, because the Indian joint family system was unknown to Ceylonese law. This plea of the defendant 1 gave rise to Conflict of Laws.

Mr Justice Rajamannar relied on Halsbury's Laws of England for the proposition that municipal courts do not entertain matters relating to title to foreign immovables, nor will they entertain any action which substantially involves the determination of such title. The learned judge had further recourse to English decision like *Deschamps v. Miller, 1901 1 Ch. 856* and the House of Lords' decision in *British South Africa Co. v. Companhia De Mozambique,*

1893, A.C. 602, to reinforce his judgment relating to the proposition that courts in any country refrain from exercising jurisdiction in matters relating to right or tile to foreign immovable properties. The learned judge had further recourse to the views of Dicey and Joseph Storey on this subject.

Accordingly, the appeal was dismissed with no order as to costs.

Part VII

LAW RELATING TO PROCEDURE

—————

The cases chosen in this part establish three fundamental principles of Conflict of Laws as set out below. They are:

(1) Whether an *ex parte* decree passed by a court of competent jurisdiction is final and binding on the parties to the case and, as such, *res judicata*.

(2) A judgment pronounced by a foreign court over persons within its jurisdiction and in a matter with which it is competent to deal, a municipal court will refrain from investigating the propriety of the proceedings in the foreign court, unless the said proceedings are prejudicial to its view of substantial justice (see Section 13 (b) of the Civil Procedure Code).

(3) The law relating to limitation of a country has no extra-territorial operation. The legal norm *ubi jus ibi*

remedium (that is, where there is right there is remedy) is subject to the law of limitation.

Janno Hassan Sait, Plaintiff, Appellant v. S.N. Mahamed Ohuthu, 1st Defendant, Respondent, 1925, Madras 155

This case established two vital principles of Conflict of Laws relating to procedure. The first one raises the question whether an *ex parte* decree passed by a court of competent jurisdiction is final and binding on the parties to the case and, as such, *res judicata*. The Division Bench of the Madras High Court, speaking through Mr Justice Phillips, held that it must be deemed to have been passed on merits based on a proper reading of Section 13 (b) of the Civil Procedure Code.

Second, the case also establishes yet another principle, as was laid down in a leading case, namely, *Pemberton v. Hughes, 1899, 1 Chancery 781*, where his Lordship, M.R. observed at page 790 as set out below:

'If a judgment is pronounced by a foreign court over persons within its jurisdiction and in a matter with which it is competent to deal, English Courts never investigate the propriety of the proceedings in the Foreign Court, unless they offend against English views of substantial justice (see Section 13 (b) of the Civil Procedure Code).

The facts of the case are as set out below:

This was a suit upon a foreign judgment of the Colombo Court against the 1st defendant. The suit was filed, in the first instance, before a second Additional Subordinate Judge of Tanjore in the year 1919. An appeal was filed against the decree of the Subordinate Judge before the District Court of Tanjore, and a second appeal was filed before the

Madras High Court challenging the decision of the District Court. The Madras High Court upheld the decision of the District Court and allowed the appeal with costs.

The 1st defendant and his brother who were trading in partnership executed a power of attorney to one Sheikh Abdul Rahiman under which he was empowered to sue in the courts in Ceylon and to appear before any court or courts of justice either as plaintiff or as defendant, and so on. The power was a very wide one that gave the agent full powers to represent the principals. The power of attorney holder Mr Abdul Rahiman in pursuance of the provisions of the power appointed one Abdul Guddus as his sub-agent during his absence from Ceylon. A suit was filed in 1915 on four promissory notes against Abdul Rahiman and Abdul Guddus. But upon their pleading that they were merely agents of the 1st defendant's firm, yet another suit was filed against the 1st defendant's firm. Notice of the suit was served on Abdul Guddus as 1st defendant's agent and the judgment on which the suit was based was passed in his absence.

Two questions arose for determination by the Court. The first question was whether the 1st defendant could be deemed to have submitted to the foreign Court in Ceylon, and, if so, he would be bound by the decision rendered by it. Mr Justice Phillips agreed with the learned district judge and held that the 1st defendant was bound by the decision of the Court in Ceylon in that, by executing a general power of attorney in favour of Abdul Rahiman who, as the agent of the 1st defendant on whose behalf he was conducting business of his principals. It was, therefore, clearly a contract binding him to appear before the Court in Ceylon and submit himself to the jurisdiction of the Court. For arriving at this conclusion Mr Justice Phillips quoted an earlier decision of the Madras Court, namely, *Ramanathan Chettiar v. Kalimuthu Pillai, ILR 1912, 37 Madras 163* (see Section 13 (b), Civil Procedure Code).

The second and the more interesting question is whether an *ex parte* decree passed by a court of competent jurisdiction, which was rendered in conformity with orderly procedure, could be deemed to have been passed on merits and, as such, *res judicata*. The Hon'ble Madras High Court answered this question in the affirmative. In this connection, it is well worth quoting Mr Justice Phillips. It runs thus: 'It is only when a defence has been raised and for some reason or another has not been adjudicated upon that the decision can be said to be not upon the merits. In other instances of *ex parte* decrees, they must be deemed to be decrees passed upon the merits'.

He further observed that 'In the present case no appearance at all was put in on behalf of the first defendant and the case was allowed to proceed *ex parte* and consequently it must be deemed to have been passed upon the merits'.

A further question was raised, namely, that the first defendant had no notice at all of the suit and that, consequently, the whole decree was a nullity as per Section 13 (d) of the Civil Procedure Code, namely, 'where the proceedings in which the judgment was obtained are opposed to natural justice'. The Hon'ble Court negatived this contention on the strength of the English decision, namely, *Pemberton v. Hughes*, where Justice Lindley, M.R. remarked, 'If a judgment is pronounced by a Foreign Court over persons within its jurisdiction and in a matter with which it is competent to deal, English Courts never investigate the propriety of the proceedings in the Foreign Court, unless they offend against English views of substantial justice' (see Section 13 of CPC).

Yet another contention on behalf of the first defendant, namely, the sub-agent Mr Abdul Guddus was unaware of the notice issued by Colombo Court and the proceedings that followed in the case before it might have been an answer to the validity of the judgment, but the same had not been shown and, consequently, the Court pronounced that the judgment was valid and binding on the first defendant.

R.A. Dickee and Co. (Agencies) Ltd., Petitioner v. The Municipal Board, Benares and Another, Opposite Party, AIR 1956, Calcutta 216

Prefatory note:

The law relating to limitation is part of the procedural law of a country and, as such, has no extra-territorial operation. It imposes a time-limit within which an action can be brought before a court seeking remedy. Such an action if instituted elsewhere will be subjected to the law of limitation of that country where the action is brought. It may or may not be time-barred in the country where the action is brought seeking remedy. The legal norm *ubi jus ibi remedium* (that is, where there is right there is remedy) is subject to the law of limitation. This short note will be perspicacious enough in our endeavour to appreciate the decision in this case.

The facts of the case, stated briefly, are as follows:

The U.P. Municipalities Act, 1916, was passed by the United Provinces Legislature (now renamed as Uttar Pradesh Legislature) under the powers conferred by Section 79 of the Government of India Act, 1915. A special law of limitation was enacted as per Sub-section (3) of Section 326 which, therefore, *pro tanto* altered and repealed the existing law of limitation. Having obtained the assent of the Governor-General-in-Council, the alteration or repeal would become valid and operative within the United Provinces as per Section 79 (2) of the Government of India Act, 1915. The assent of the Governor-General, however, would not authorize the United Provinces Legislature to alter or repeal the Indian law of Limitation in respect of other provinces of India. Sub-section 3 of Section 326 would, therefore, not apply to a suit instituted in a court outside the United Provinces. Accordingly, the word 'action' in Section 326 (3) of the U.P. Municipalities Act ought to be construed as meaning 'action' brought within the United Provinces. In this case, a suit was instituted against the Municipal Board, Benares, in a Court of Small Causes, Calcutta, for recovery of the price of goods said to have been sold and delivered by the plaintiff-petitioner to the Municipal Board, Benares. Four items of goods were dispatched by the plaintiff by train from Calcutta to Benares to the Municipal Board, Benares, of which two items of goods were rejected on the ground of late supply and inferiority of quality. The learned judge of the Court of Small Causes by his judgment, dated 12 May 1952, dismissed the suit on the ground that it was barred by the special law of limitation of the United Provinces Municipalities Act, 1916 (Act II of 1916). The judgment was affirmed by a Full Bench of the Court of Small Causes on 2 February 1954. The plaintiff-petitioner, thereupon, filed a revision petition to the Calcutta High Court, challenging the decision of the Court of Small Causes that the special law of limitation of U.P. made the suit time-barred.

The Calcutta High Court reversed the finding of the Court of Small Causes, Calcutta, that the suit was barred by the special law of limitation of U.P. on the mistaken assumption that it had extra-territorial operation. On the contrary, the suit was not barred by the law of limitation. Article 52 of the Indian Law of limitation would then apply to the case. Therefore, on the basis of the said finding, the Calcutta High Court remitted the suit to the learned judge of the Court of Small Causes for re-trial and disposal according to law. While so disposing of the case. Mr Justice Bachawat of the Division Bench of the High Court made the following observation: 'The law of the country of origin determines the power and functions of the corporation and the *lex fori* must look to that law for the determination of such questions' (see para 21 of the judgment).

The Court further observed, on the basis of the rules of Conflict of Laws, as set out below:

A special law of procedure and a special law of limitation applicable to the corporation by the laws of the country of its origin cannot however be said to be part of the attributes of the juristic personality of the corporation. The corporation does not carry with it the special law of limitation and the special law of procedure when it sues or (be) sued in another country. Just as a natural person does not carry the laws of limitation and the special laws of procedure of his country of origin when he goes to another country (see para 22 of the judgment).

In sum, the review could be wound up with a terse observation, such as how could we credit judges of the lower courts with any knowledge of the basics of the rules of conflict of laws!

GLOSSARY OF LATIN TERMS

---

ab initio	'from the beginning or inception'.
animo et facto	An intention to make the new place one's abode coupled with an actual transfer of bodily presence from one place to another.
audi alteram partem	'Hear the other side', or no man should be condemned unheard or both the sides must be heard before passing any order.
brutum fulmen	It is used to indicate either an empty threat, or a judgement at law which has no practical effect.
de facto	'Existing in fact, whether legally recognized or not, an expression indicating the actual state of circumstances independently of any question of right or title'.

ex facie	'On the face of it'. It is a legal term typically used to note that a document's explicit terms are defective without further investigation.
ex contractu	'From a contract', one source of causes of actions.
ex delicto	'From wrong', 'from tort', the whole class of private actions that are not ex contractu.
ex parte	'From a side', it refers to a proceeding that involves only one of the parties to a lawsuit.
fait accompli	'A thing which is done or accomplished'; a completed act.
habeas corpus	'You should have the body', a writ to bring a prisoner out of prison for trial or release.
in absentem	'In absence'. Its meaning varies by jurisdiction and legal system. In common law legal systems, the phrase is more than a spatial description. It suggests recognition of violation to a defendant's right to be present in court proceedings in a criminal trial.
in forma pauperis	'In pauper's form'. An abbreviation of court documents and records granted to a poor petitioner; or without court costs.
in limine	'At the outset'. Preliminary, in law referring to a motion that is made to the judge before or during trial, often about the admissibility of evidence believed prejudicial.
In re	'In the matter of'. The beginning of a court document's title.

inter alia	'Among other things'. A term used in formal extract minutes to indicate that the minute quoted has been taken from a fuller record of other matters, or when alluding to the parent group after quoting a particular example.
ipso facto	'By the fact itself', without further process. For example, the signing of a will before witnesses makes a will valid 'ipso facto', without registration or deposit.
lex causae	'Law of the cause'. In conflict of laws, lex causae is the law chosen by the forum court from the relevant legal systems when it judges an international or inter-jurisdictional case. It refers to the usage of particular local laws as the basis or "cause" for the ruling.
lex fori	'Law of the court' hearing the case.
lex loci celebrationis	'Law of the place where the marriage is celebrated'.
lex loci delicti commissi	'Law of the place where the delict [tort] was committed'.
lex domicilii	'Law of the domicile' of the defendant.
lex patriae	'Law of the fatherland, in modern usage, nationality law'. In conflict of laws, is the system of public law applied to a lawsuit if a choice is to be made between two or more laws that would change the outcome.
lex situs	'The law of the place in which property is situated for the purposes of the Conflict of laws'.

mutatis mutandis	'With those things changed that should be changed', 'with the necessary modifications'. For example, a contract of lease of a horse and wagon will serve, mutatis mutandis, for the lease of a truck.
non obstante	'Notwithstanding clause'. A legislative device which is usually employed to give overriding effect to certain provisions over some contrary provision that may be found either in the same enactment, or some other enactment, that is to say, to avoid the operation and defect of all contrary provisions.
parens patriae	'Parent of the nation'. A public policy requiring courts to protect the best interests of any child involved in a lawsuit.
per se	'Through itself'. Without referring to anything else, intrinsically, taken without qualifications, etc. A common example is negligence per se.
prima facie	'At first appearance', 'presumably'. A prima facie case is sufficient argument and evidence by the plaintiff or prosecutor to stand unless overcome by the defendant. It discharges and transfers the burden of proof.
pro tanto	'For that much, to that extent, for so much, for as much as may be', compensation for an expropriation without prejudice to a claim for more.

res ipsa loquitur	'The thing speaks for itself'. A phrase from the common law of torts meaning that negligence can be inferred from the fact that such an accident happened, without proof of exactly how.
res judicata	'Judged thing'. A matter which has been decided by a court. Often refers to the legal concept that once a matter has been finally decided by the courts, it cannot be litigated again.
situs	'Place' as a legal characteristic.
ubi jus ibi remedium	'where there is right, there is a remedy'.

INDEX

About the Author

———

V.C. Govindaraj is a former professor in the Faculty of Law of the University of Delhi in the years 1959–93. He taught subjects such as constitutional law and international law, public and private law, Roman law, law of international institutions and human rights, law of the sea, and other allied courses in public international law. He earned his doctoral degree from the University of Delhi in 1988 while being engaged as a faculty member in teaching and guiding students in their research activities.

Prior to his joining the Faculty of Law, University of Delhi, in the year 1959, he earned his master's degree in economics and in international law and constitutional law from the University of Madras. He practised law in the years 1953–8 in the High Court of Judicature at Madras. For a year or so he was a research scholar in the

Department of International and Constitutional Law at the University of Madras under the guidance of Professor C.H. Alexandrowicz, the then visiting professor of the University of Madras. His academic activities range from being a visiting scholar at the School of Law, Columbia University, New York, in the years 1969–70, sponsored by Ford Foundation, to an assistant director of research, Public International Law, in the Asian–African Legal Consultative Committee, New Delhi, in the years 1972–4 on deputation from the University of Delhi; he was a senior research fellow on human rights at the School of Law, Columbia University, during 1989–90, sponsored again by Ford Foundation. He has been a visiting professor at various prestigious academic institutions such as the National Law School of India University, Bangalore, Jawaharlal Nehru University, New Delhi, and many others.